P9-CBD-935

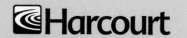

PHONICS
Practice Book

Grade 1

Harcourt

Orlando   Boston   Dallas   Chicago   San Diego

Visit *The Learning Site!*
www.harcourtschool.com

ISBN 0-15-313559-X

14 15 073 2006 2005 2004

CONTENTS

Unit 1: Consonants

Harcourt

Harcourt

Unit 2: Digraphs

Unit 3: Consonant Blends

Unit 4: Short Vowels

Unit 5: Long Vowels

Phonics Practice Book

Harcourt

Unit 6: *R-Controlled Vowels and Vowel Variants*

Unit 7: Contractions

Harcourt

Unit 8: Inflected Endings

Cut-Out Fold-Up Books

Phonics Practice Book

Harcourt

Name _____

Help the  get to the . Color the pictures whose names begin or end with the sound /m/.

Harcourt

Name _____

Say the name of each picture. Write **m** in the box that shows where you hear the sound in each word—at the beginning, in the middle, or at the end.

1	2	3

m | | | | | m | | | | | m

4	5	6

7	8	9

Initial, Medial, and Final Consonant: / m / m   Phonics Practice Book

Harcourt

Name _____

Say the name of each picture. Color the pictures whose names begin or end with the sound /s/.

Initial and Final Consonant: / s / • Phonemic Awareness

Harcourt

Say the name of each picture. Write **s** in the box or boxes that show where you hear the sound in each word—at the beginning, in the middle, or at the end.

1				2				3			
S				S	S						S

4			5			6		

7			8			9		

$$\begin{array}{r} 2 \\ +1 \\ \hline 3 \end{array}$$

Harcourt

Name _____

Say the name of each picture. Color the pictures whose names begin or end with the sound /t/.

Phonics Practice Book   Initial and Final Consonant: / t /   •   Phonemic Awareness

13

Name _____

Say the name of each picture. Write **t** in the box or boxes that show where you hear the sound in each word—at the beginning, in the middle, or at the end.

1	2	3

t					t						t

4	5	6

7	8	9

Initial, Medial, and Final Consonant: / t / t   Phonics Practice Book

Name _____

Say the name of each picture. Color the pictures whose names begin with the sound /k/.

Harcourt

Initial Consonant: / k /   •   Phonemic Awareness

Name _____

Say the name of each picture. Write **c** in the box or boxes that show where you hear the sound in each word—at the beginning, in the middle, or at the end.

1	2	3

C					C			C	C

4	5	6

7	8	9

Initial, Medial, and Final Consonant: / k / c

Phonics Practice Book

Name _____

Say the name of each picture. Color the pictures whose names begin or end with the sound /p/.

Say the name of each picture. Write **p** in the box or boxes that show where you hear the sound in each word—at the beginning, in the middle, or at the end.

1	2	3

p | | | | | p | p | | | | p

4	5	6

7	8	9

Harcourt

Name _____

Say the name of each picture. Color the pictures whose names begin with the sound /h/.

hat

Say the name of each picture. If it begins with the sound /h/, write **h** on the lines.

1	2	3
h		

4	5	6

7	8	9

10	11	12

Harcourt

Name _____

Say the name of each picture. Circle the letter that stands for its beginning sound.

1	2	3
t s c	p h m	s p c

4	5	6
m t h	t c p	s h c

7	8	9
p m h	s t c	t h p

10	11	12
c t m	p h s	s t m

Phonics Practice Book

Review of Consonants: m, s, t, c, p, h

21

Name _____

Say the name of each picture. Write the letter that stands for its beginning or ending sound. Then trace the rest of the word.

1	2	3
sat	_at_	_ca_

4	5	6
_ma_	_ap_	_at_

7	8	9
_at_	_ha_	_ap_

Harcourt

Name _____

Say the name of each picture. Write the word on the lines.

1		_map_
2		
3		
4		
5		
6		

Harcourt

Name _____

Say the name of each picture. Circle the letter that stands for a sound you hear in the middle. Then write the letter.

1 s t (m) m	**2** t c p	**3** s c m
4 p c t	**5** s p m	**6** p s m
7 t s c	**8** m s p	**9** c m t

Review of Medial Consonants: *m, s, t, c, p*   Phonics Practice Book

Name _____

Say the name of each picture. Color the pictures whose names begin or end with the sound /d/.

Harcourt

Name _____

Say the name of each picture. Write **d** in the box that shows where you hear the sound in each word—at the beginning, in the middle, or at the end.

1	2	3

4	5	6

7	8	9

Initial, Medial, and Final Consonant: / d / d   Phonics Practice Book

Name _____

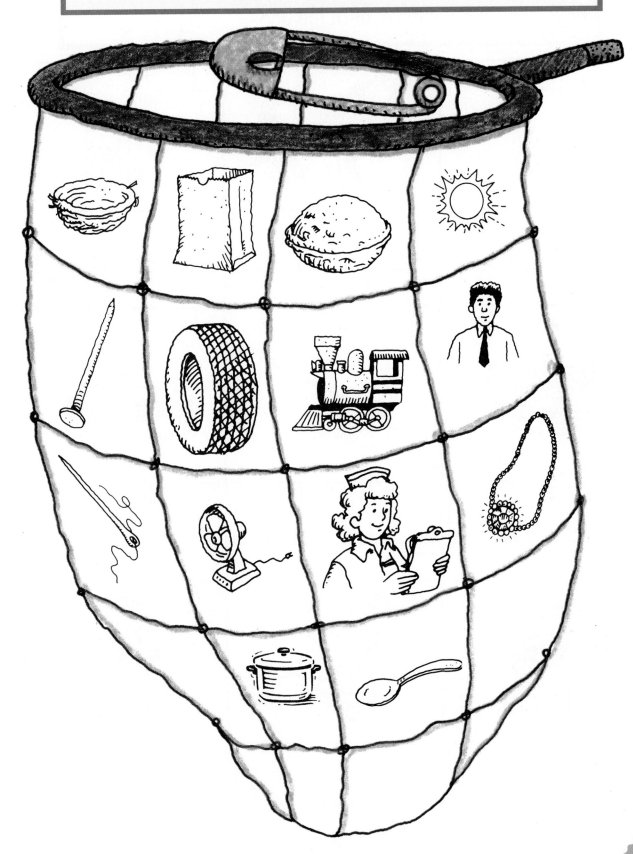

Harcourt

Say the name of each picture. Write **n** in the box that shows where you hear the sound in each word—at the beginning, in the middle, or at the end.

28

Initial, Medial, and Final Consonant: / n / n

Phonics Practice Book

Name _____

Say the name of each picture. Color the pictures whose names begin or end with the sound /k/.

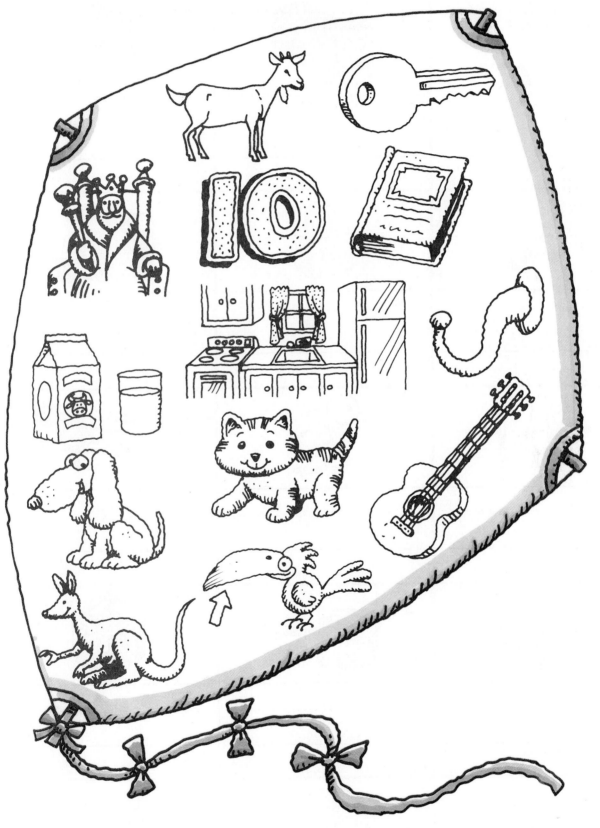

Harcourt

Name _____

tack

Say the name of each picture. If it ends with the sound /k/, write **ck** on the lines.

1	2	3
ck		
4	5	6
7	8	9
10	11	12

Harcourt

Say the name of each picture. Color the pictures whose names begin or end with the sound /l/.

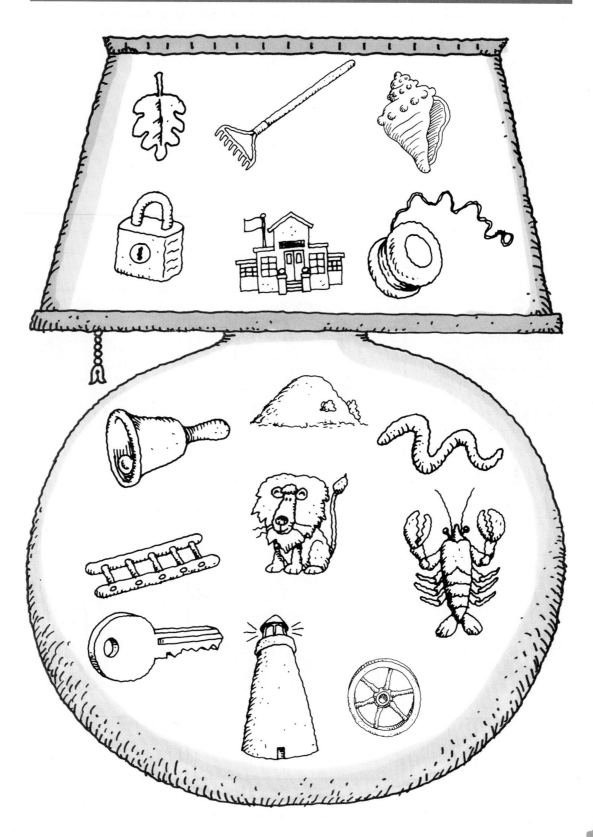

Name _____

Say the name of each picture. Write **l** in the box that shows where you hear the sound in each word—at the beginning, in the middle, or at the end.

1

2

3

4

5

6

7

8

9

Initial, Medial, and Final Consonant: / l / / l /

Phonics Practice Book

Name _____

ball

Say the name of each picture. If it ends with the sound /l/, write **ll** on the lines.

1	2	3
4	5	6
7	8	9
10	11	12

Harcourt

Say the name of each picture. Circle the beginning letter.

1	2	3
k n l	d n k	l d n
4	5	6
k l d	l n d	n k d
7	8	9
k n l	d l k	l n d
10	11	12
n k d	l d k	n k l

Review of Consonants: *d, n, k, l*

Phonics Practice Book

Harcourt

Say the name of each picture. Write the letter that stands for its beginning or ending sound. Then trace the whole word.

1	2	3
_____ pi	_____ id	_____ ap

4	5	6
_____ pa	_____ pa	_____ iss

7	8	9
_____ ca	_____ ad	_____ sa

Harcourt

Name _____

Say the name of each picture. Circle the letter that stands for the sound you hear in the middle. Then write the letter.

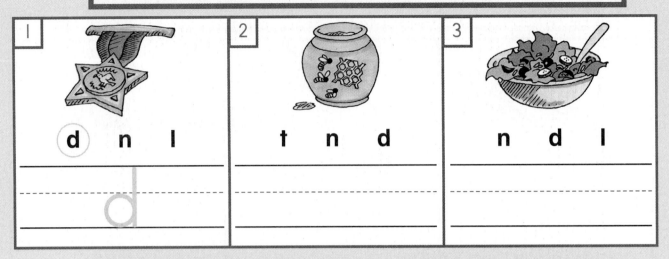

1	2	3
(d) n l	t n d	n d l
d		

Say the name of each picture. Circle the letters that stand for the sound you hear at the end. Then write the letters.

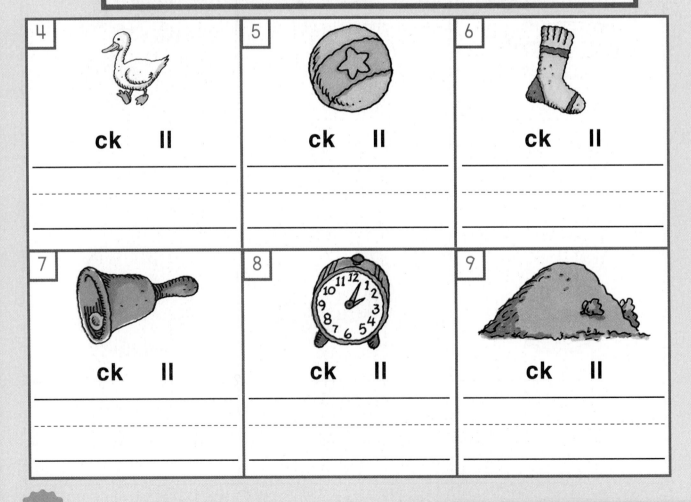

4	5	6
ck ll	ck ll	ck ll

7	8	9
ck ll	ck ll	ck ll

36   Review of Consonants: *d, n, l, ll, ck*

Phonics Practice Book

Harcourt

Name _____

Help the 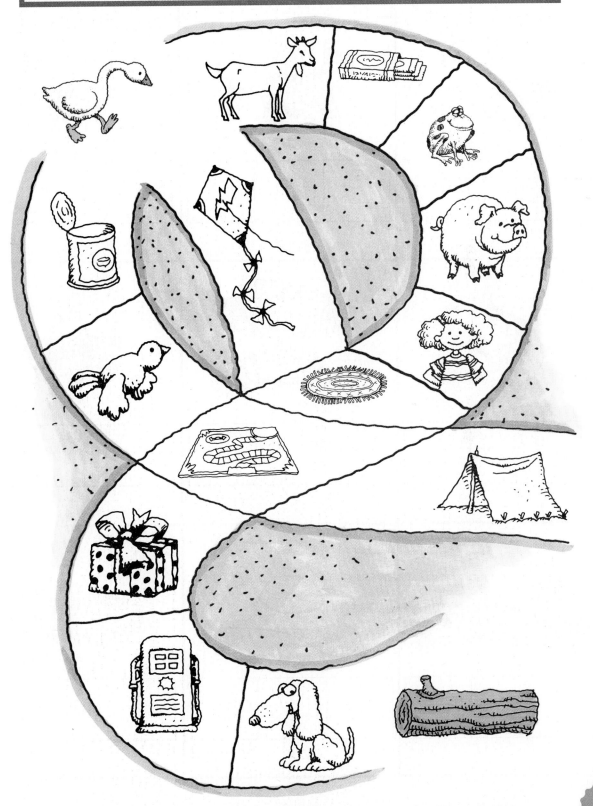 get to the ▬. Color the pictures
whose names begin or end with the sound /g/.

Harcourt

Name _____

Say the name of each picture. Write **g** in the box that shows where you hear the sound in each word—at the beginning, in the middle, or at the end.

1	2	3

4	5	6

7	8	9

Initial, Medial, and Final Consonant: / g / g

Phonics Practice Book

Name _____

Color each picture whose name ends like the name of the child at the left of the box.

1. **Todd**

2. **Matt**

3. **Cass**

4. **Ann**

Final Consonants: / s / *ss*, / t / *tt*, / d / *dd*, / n / *nn*

Look at the pictures. Read the sentences. Write letters from the box to complete the words.

ss   dd   tt   nn

1		Todd has a __mi_____.
2		Cass is at an ___i_____.
3		Matt can __a_____.
4		Ann will not __mi____.

Double Consonants: / s / *ss,* / t / *tt,* / d / *dd,* / n / *nn*

Phonics Practice Book

Harcourt

Say the name of each picture. Color the pictures whose names begin with the sound /r/.

Initial Consonant: / r / • Phonemic Awareness

41

ring

Say the name of each picture. If it begins with the sound /r/, write **r** on the lines.

1	2	3
r		

4	5	6

7	8	9

10	11	12

Initial Consonant: / r / r

Phonics Practice Book

Harcourt

Name _____

Say the name of each picture. Color the pictures whose names begin or end with the sound /f/.

Initial and Final Consonant: / f /   •   Phonemic Awareness

Say the name of each picture. Write **f** in the box that shows where you hear the sound in each word—at the beginning or at the end.

1
f |

2
 | f

3
 |

4
 |

5
 |

6
 |

7
 |

8
 |

Initial and Final Consonant: / f / f

Phonics Practice Book

Harcourt

Name _____

 o**ff**

Color the pictures whose names end with the sound /f/. Write **ff** under those pictures.

1	2
_____ - - - - - - - - - - - _____	_____ - - - - - - - - - - - _____

3	4
_____ - - - - - - - - - - - _____	_____ - - - - - - - - - - - _____

Harcourt

Say the name of each picture. Color the pictures whose names begin or end with the sound /b/.

Initial and Final Consonant: / b / • Phonemic Awareness   Phonics Practice Book

Say the name of each picture. Write **b** in the box or boxes that show where you hear the sound in each word—at the beginning, in the middle, or at the end.

1

b		

2

b	b	

3

		b

4

5

6

7

8

9

Harcourt

Name _____

Say the name of each picture. Color the pictures whose names begin with the sound /w/.

Initial Consonant: / w / • Phonemic Awareness

Phonics Practice Book

Harcourt

Name _____

wagon

Say the name of each picture. If it begins
with the sound /w/, write **w** on the lines.

1	2	3

W

4	5	6

7	8	9

10	11	12

Harcourt

Help the  find his friend . Color the pictures whose names end with the sound /ks/.

Final Consonant: / ks /   •   Phonemic Awareness

Phonics Practice Book

o**x**

Say the name of each picture. If it ends with the sound /ks/, write **x** on the lines.

1 _____ - - - X - - - _____	**2** _____ - - - - - - - _____	**3** _____ - - - - - - - _____
4 _____ - - - - - - - _____	**5** _____ - - - - - - - _____	**6** _____ - - - - - - - _____
7 _____ - - - - - - - _____	**8** _____ - - - - - - - _____	**9** _____ - - - - - - - _____

Name _____

Write the letter or letters that complete each word. Then trace the rest of the word.

1	2	3
___ock	___si	___e

4	5	6
___o	___a	___i

Say the name of each picture. Circle the letter that stands for the sound you hear in the middle. Then write the letter.

7	8	9
g b f	g f b	f g b

Harcourt

Name _____

Say the name of each picture. Write the word on the lines.

1		fix
2		
3		
4		

Say the name of each picture. Write the letters that stand for the beginning and middle sounds.

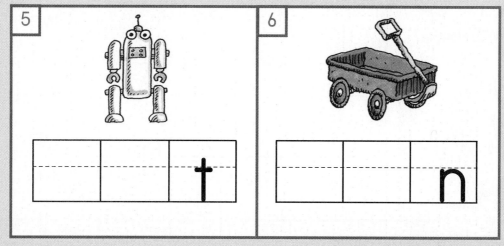

5

6

t

n

Harcourt

Name _____

Look at each picture. Circle the word that completes the sentence. Then write the word.

1		What a big _____ _____ _____!	wall web cab
2		_____ _____ See Rex _____.	wag log win
3		What is in this _____ _____ _____?	bag fox box
4		_____ _____ It is _____.	red rip wet
5		_____ _____ It _____ Rex!	fans rips fits

Review of Consonants: *g, r, f, b, w, x*

Phonics Practice Book

Harcourt

Name _____

Look at each picture. Circle the word that completes the sentence. Then write the word.

1		This is my _____ .	miss mitt
2		She can _____ .	add all
3		I see the _____ .	odd inn
4		He gets a _____ .	kiss hill
5		Mick likes to _____ .	hiss sniff

Review of Double Consonants: *ss, tt, dd, nn, ff*

Name _____

yak

Help the 🐂 get home. Color the pictures whose names begin with the sound /y/.

Name _____

<u>y</u>ak

Say the name of each picture. If it begins with the sound /y/, write **y** on the lines.

1	2	3
y		
4	5	6
7	8	9

Harcourt

Say the name of each picture. Color the pictures whose names begin with the sound /j/.

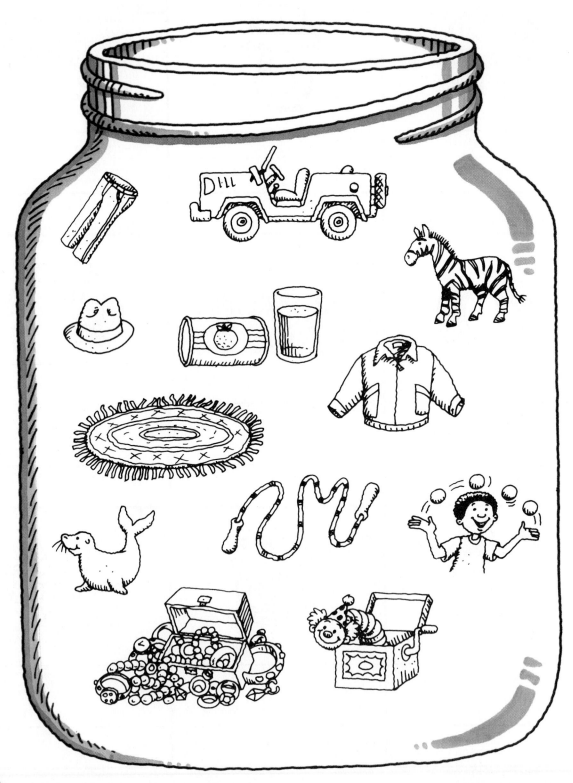

Initial Consonant: / j /   •   Phonemic Awareness

Phonics Practice Book

jar

Say the name of each picture. If it begins with the sound /j/, write **j** on the lines.

1	2	3
j		

4	5	6

7	8	9

10	11	12

Harcourt

Name _____

Help the  get the 🐝. Color the pictures whose names begin or end with the sound /z/.

Initial and Final Consonant: / z /   •   Phonemic Awareness

Phonics Practice Book

zebra

buzz

Say the name of each picture. If it begins with the sound /z/, write **z.** If it ends with the sound /z/, write **zz.**

1	2	3
z		

4	5	6

7	8	9

Harcourt

Initial and Final Consonant: / z / z, zz

Name _____

Say the name of each picture. Color the pictures whose names begin with the sound /v/.

Initial Consonant: / v / • Phonemic Awareness

Phonics Practice Book

Harcourt

Say the name of each picture. Write **v** in the box that shows where you hear the sound in each word—at the beginning or in the middle.

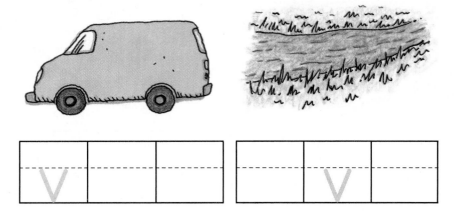

| v | | | | | v | |

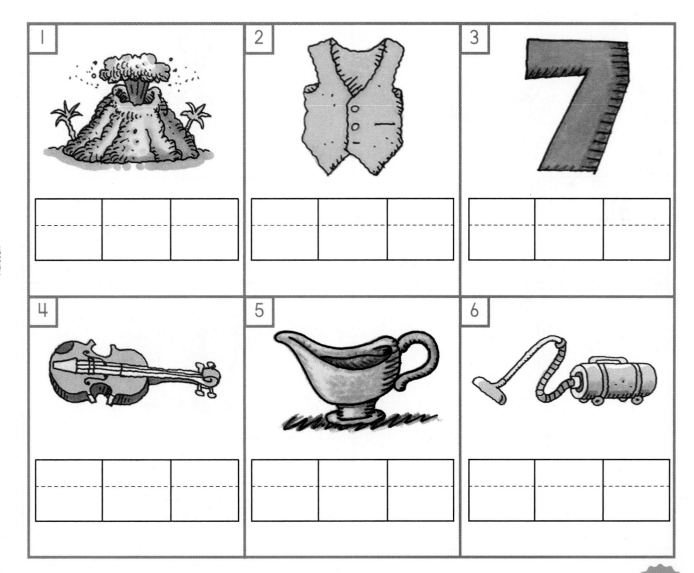

Harcourt

Name _____

Write the letter or letters that complete each word. Then trace the rest of the word.

1
_____

- - - - - - - - - - -

an

2
_____

- - - - - - - - - - -

et

3
_____

- - - - - - - - - - -

arn

4
_____

- - - - - - - - - - -

ip

5
_____

- - - - - - - - - - -

ar

6
_____

- - - - - - - - - - -

ak

Harcourt

64 Review of Consonants: y, j, z, v

Phonics Practice Book

Name _____

Look at each picture. Circle the word that completes the sentence. Then write the word.

1		_____ - - - - - - - - - - - - - - - Here is your _____.	yarn vest jam
2		_____ - - - - - - - - - - - - - - - I will _____ it.	yes van zip
3		_____ - - - - - - - - - - - - - - - My hat has _____.	mitt fuzz puff
4		_____ - - - - - - - - - - - - - - - We play in the _____.	yard jazz vent
5		_____ - - - - - - - - - - - - - - - I see a _____.	zip yak jet

Write the letter that completes the word. Then trace the rest of the word.

6	7	_____ - - - - - - - - - - - - - - - s e _ e n

Review of Consonants: *y, j, z, zz, v*   65

Name _____

Say the name of each picture. Color the pictures whose names begin or end with the sound /s/.

Initial and Final Consonant: / s /   •   Phonemic Awareness

Phonics Practice Book

Name _____

city

Say the name of each picture. If it begins with the sound /s/, write **c** on the lines.

1	2	3
c		

4	5	6

7	8	9

Harcourt

Name _____

Help the  find the . Color the pictures whose
names begin or end with the sound /j/.

Initial and Final Consonant: / j /   •   Phonemic Awareness   Phonics Practice Book

Harcourt

Name _____

gem

Say the name of each picture. If it begins with the sound /j/, write **g** on the lines.

1	2	3
_____ _____	_____ _____	_____ _____
g		
4	5	6
_____ _____	_____ _____	_____ _____
7	8	9
_____ _____	_____ _____	_____ _____

Harcourt

Phonics Practice Book

Initial Consonant: / j / g

69

Name _____

Say the name of each picture. Write **c** or **g** to show the letter that stands for the beginning sound.

Write the letter that completes each word. Then trace the rest of the word.

4	5	6
brid e	ircle	dan e

7	8	9
em	mi e	sta e

Review of Consonants: / s / c; / j / g, dge

Phonics Practice Book

Name _____

Say the name of each picture. Write the letters that stand for the beginning and ending sounds.

1			2			3		
p	g							

4			5			6		

7			8			9		

10			11			12		

Cumulative Review of Consonants

Name _____

Circle and write the letter or letters that complete each word. Then trace the rest of the word.

1	x s n	2	m t c	3	t d p
	bu___		___ar		___esk

4	v b m	5	f t d	6	ss ff zz
	se___en		be___		ki___

7	m n b	8	b l p	9	f v k
	___et		___na ___kin		___an

10	k p t	11	w h y	12	nn ff tt
	___ick		___arn		i___

Cumulative Review of Consonants

Phonics Practice Book

Harcourt

Name _____

Circle and write the letter or letters that complete each word. Then trace the rest of the word.

1	dd ff tt	a___

2	ck ss ll	do___

3	l t b	ci___ y

4	z g k	em___

5	ff ll tt	mi___

6	ck zz ff	bu___

7	m d g	ca___

8	w g c	___ircle

9	ck zz ff	so___

10	m s d	ba___ket

11	ff tt nn	pu___

12	m l b	sa___ ad

Harcourt

Name _____

 Read the rhymes. Then use a word or words from them to complete each sentence.

The duck and the pig
had fun with a wig.

The seal and the dog
went to a city in the fog.

The fox got a hit,
but the cub had his mitt.

The camel and the yak
had fudge for a snack.

_____

1.   The pig put on a _____ .

_____

2.   The dog went to the _____ .

_____

3.   The cub had a _____ .

_____

4.   The _____ and the yak ate

_____

_____ .

Cumulative Review of Consonants   phonics Practice Book

Name _____

Fill in the circle next to the letter or letters that complete each word. Write the letters. Then trace the rest of the word.

1	○ d ○ p ○ t	2	○ ck ○ tt ○ ll	3	○ v ○ f ○ h
	cu		hi		ox

4	○ m ○ p ○ b	5	○ m ○ s ○ r	6	○ s ○ b ○ n
le	on		ug		ga

7	○ r ○ l ○ t	8	○ p ○ n ○ c	9	○ d ○ b ○ f
	ock		ca tus		all

10	○ d ○ n ○ t	11	○ f ○ c ○ g	12	○ j ○ p ○ t
	sa		ity		en

Harcourt

Name _____

 CHECK-UP

Fill in the circle next to the letter or letters that complete each word. Write the letters. Then trace the rest of the word.

1	○ w ○ s ○ r	2	○ n ○ b ○ t	3	○ ss ○ ll ○ ff
	eb		ca		o

4	○ z ○ c ○ m	5	○ s ○ n ○ v	6	○ s ○ h ○ g
	ap		si ter		um

7	○ ff ○ ck ○ nn	8	○ f ○ n ○ c	9	○ y ○ b ○ l
	tru		est		ard

10	○ b ○ m ○ g	11	○ g ○ h ○ z	12	○ s ○ j ○ v
	wa on		em		un

Harcourt

Fill in the circle next to the letter or letters that complete each word. Write the letters. Then trace the rest of the word.

1	6	○ d ○ x ○ p	_____ si

2	(cat)	○ c ○ g ○ m	_____ at

3	(mother and child)	○ k ○ t ○ d	_____ iss

4	(zipper)	○ b ○ s ○ z	_____ ipper

5	(hat)	○ y ○ m ○ h	_____ at

6	(medal)	○ n ○ d ○ g	me _____ al

7	(frog)	○ g ○ d ○ s	fro _____

8	(vest)	○ b ○ v ○ w	_____ est

9	(bib)	○ x ○ b ○ f	_____ ib

10	(wagon)	○ d ○ g ○ p	wa _____ on

11	(jet)	○ j ○ r ○ s	_____ et

12	(mitt)	○ ss ○ ll ○ tt	mi _____

Harcourt

Draw a line from each picture to the sentence that tells about it.

1

The cat gets the yarn.

The dog has the bat.

The dog is in the box.

2

Jim has a wagon.

Jeff cuts a melon.

Jack gets the salad.

3

They buzz by a truck.

They buzz over grass.

They buzz by a wall.

4

Val zips up her vest.

Pam sees a big yak.

Ann has a pretty gem.

5

Derek likes the city.

James turns the page.

Josef calls his mom.

Color each picture whose name begins with the sound /th/.

1	2	3
	10	30

4	5	6

7	8	9
13		

Harcourt

Name _____

Color each picture whose name ends with the sound /th/.

1	2	3
4	5	6
7	8	9

Final Digraph: / th /   •   Phonemic Awareness   Phonics Practice Book

think

Say the name of each picture. If it begins with the sound /th/, write **th** on the lines.

1	2	3
th		

4	5	6

7	8	9

Harcourt

ba<u>th</u>

Say the name of each picture. If it ends with the sound /th/, write **th** on the lines.

1	2	3
th		

4	5	6

7	8	9

Final Digraph: / th / *th*

Phonics Practice Book

Harcourt

Name _____

Look at each picture. Circle the word that completes the sentence. Then write the word.

1		
	_____ - Is _____ your cat?	thick that the
2		
	_____ - I will pick _____ cat.	the this that

father

Say the name of each picture. If it has the sound /th/ in the middle, write **th** on the lines.

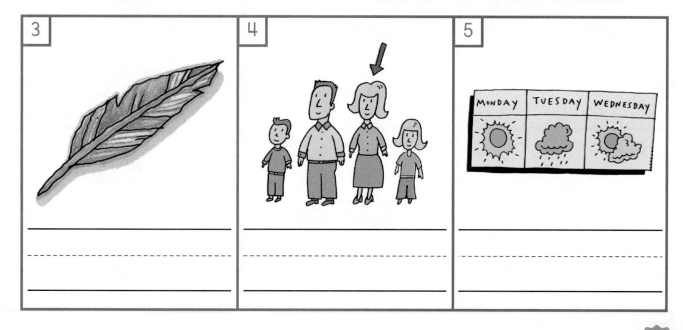

3	4	5
_____ - - - - - - - - - _____	_____ - - - - - - - - - _____	_____ - - - - - - - - - _____

Name _____

Color each picture whose name begins with the sound /sh/.

Initial Digraph: / sh / • Phonemic Awareness

Phonics Practice Book

Harcourt

Color each picture whose name ends with the sound /sh/.

1	2	3
4	5	6
7	8	9

Name _____

ship

Say the name of each picture. If it begins with the sound /sh/, write **sh** on the lines.

1	2	3
sh		

4	5	6

7	8	9

10	11	12

Initial Digraph: / sh / *sh*

Phonics Practice Book

Harcourt

di<u>sh</u>

Say the name of each picture. If it ends with the sound /sh/, write **sh** on the lines.

1 sh	2	3
4	5	6
7	8	9
10	11	12

Name _____

Say the name of each picture. Circle the letters that stand for a sound you hear in the word. Then write the letters in the box that shows where you hear the sound—at the beginning, in the middle, or at the end.

1		2		3	
	sh ff (th)		th sh dd		zz sh th

4		5		6	
	ss th sh		th tt sh		sh ck th

7		8		9	
	th sh tt		nn th sh		th sh ss

Harcourt

Name _____

Write **th** or **sh** to complete each picture name. Then trace the rest of the word.

1	2	3
di	mo	ba

4	5	6
in	pa	tra

7	8	9
ip	ink	fi

Harcourt

Color each picture whose name begins with the sound /ch/.

1	2	3
4	5	6
7	8	9
10	11	12

Initial Digraph: / ch / • Phonemic Awareness

Phonics Practice Book

Harcourt

Color each picture whose name ends with the sound /ch/.

1	2	3
4	5	6
7	8	9

Final Digraph: / ch / • Phonemic Awareness

Harcourt

Name _____

chest

Say the name of each picture. If it begins with the sound /ch/, write **ch.** Then trace the rest of the word.

1	2	3
est	ap	eck

4	5	6
ip	op	ing

7	8	9
ick	in	ips

Initial Digraph: / ch / *ch*

Phonics Practice Book

Harcourt

Say the name of each picture. If it ends with the sound /ch/, write **tch.** Then trace the rest of the word.

ma<u>tch</u>

1		2		3	
pa		pi		ki	
4		5		6	
ma		ta		ca	

Say the name of each picture. If it ends with the sound /ch/, write **ch.** Then trace the rest of the word.

pea<u>ch</u>

7		8		9	
ben		du		bran	

Color each picture whose name ends with the sound /l/.

1	2	3
4	5	6
7	8	9
10	11	12

Final Digraph: / l / • Phonemic Awareness

Phonics Practice Book

Harcourt

Write **le** to complete each word. Then draw a line from the word to the picture it names.

1	sadd	
2	pick	
3	kett	
4	app	
5	bott	

Harcourt

Color each picture whose name begins with the sounds /kw/.

1	2	3

4	5	6

7	8	9
	Quack!	

Initial Digraph: / kw /   •   Phonemic Awareness

Phonics Practice Book

Harcourt

Name _____

quack

Say the name of each picture. If it begins with the sounds /kw/, write **qu** on the lines.

1	2	3
Quack!		
qu		

4	5	6
		JUICE 1 QUART

7	8	9

Harcourt

Name _____

Circle and write the letters that complete each picture name. Then trace the rest of the word.

1		le tch sh	2		ch k qu	3		th ch qu
	pa ___			ilt			op

4		le ch sh	5		ck ch qu	6		ch t th
	pick ___			ick			ben

7	Quack!	k ch qu	8		th ch le	9		t tch ck
	ack			app			ca

10		qu ch ck	11		t th ch	12		th le ch
	in			bran			bott

Review of Digraphs: *ch, tch, le, qu*

Phonics Practice Book

Name _____

Read the story. Then answer the questions.

"Let's set up the lunch," said Trish.

"We have two quarts of punch and some chips to nibble," said Dan.

"We have a big sandwich with pickles, chicken, and some apples," said Mom.

"Now all we need is Mitch," said Trish.

"Quick! Let's finish," said Dan. "Here come Mitch and Dad!"

"We missed you, Mitch!" said Mom, Dan, and Trish.

1. What did Mom, Dan, and Trish fix for Mitch?

_____

_____

_____

2. What would you eat if you were at this lunch?

_____

_____

_____

Harcourt

Name _____

Color each picture whose name begins with the sound /hw/.

1	2	3
4	5	6
7	8	9

Initial Digraph: / hw / • Phonemic Awareness

Phonics Practice Book

Harcourt

Name _____

whale

Say the name of each picture. If it begins with the sound /hw/, write **wh**. Then trace the rest of the word.

1	2
_____ ale	_____ isper

3	4
_____ ick	_____ ite

5	6
_____ ell	_____ een

7	8
_____ eel	_____ iskers

Harcourt

Name _____

Circle and write the letters that complete each picture name. Then trace the rest of the word.

1 ch / sh / wh ___ick	**2** wh / sh / qu ___ilt	**3** wh / th / sh ___ba ___
4 th / sh / ch fi ___	**5** ch / sh / th ben ___	**6** sh / ch / qu ___ip
7 sh / th / wh ___ale	**8** le / ch / qu app ___	**9** wh / sh / th ___eel
10 tch / le / th pi ___	**11** sh / wh / th ___ell	**12** wh / th / sh ___irty

Cumulative Review of Digraphs   Phonics Practice Book

Name _____

SUPER REVIEW

1. Which chick is in a bath? Make a brush for him.

2. Find the chick with the itch on her chin. Write **tch** on her.

3. Chip chats with Dan. Dan quacks. Write **ch** on Chip.

4. A chick will hatch soon! Write **sh** on the shell.

5. Chuck will catch the white one. Write **wh** by it.

6. Chad went to the little shed. Make a path to the shed.

Harcourt

Name _____

 CHECK-UP

Fill in the circle next to the name of each picture.

1		2		3	
	○ shop ○ chop ○ crop		○ catch ○ cattle ○ cash		○ patch ○ path ○ past

4		5		6	
	○ sip ○ ship ○ whip		○ bath ○ beach ○ beak		○ chick ○ thick ○ quick

7		8		9	
	○ bath ○ batch ○ bottle		○ thin ○ chin ○ shin		○ needle ○ neat ○ need

10		11		12	
	○ fish ○ fifth ○ fetch		○ kettle ○ chill ○ quilt		○ quail ○ whale ○ shell

Digraphs Test

Phonics Practice Book

Harcourt

Fill in the circle next to the sentence that goes with each picture.

1.
   - ○ Show me your white shell.
   - ○ Why is your sandwich so thick?
   - ○ What did you pitch in the trash?

2.
   - ○ We have to rush to the ship.
   - ○ We have to check the fish.
   - ○ We have to dash to catch the bus.

3.
   - ○ They brush the dog's chin.
   - ○ It's time for a quick bath.
   - ○ The dog can catch an apple.

4.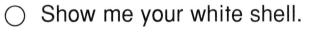
   - ○ This dish is for the chicks.
   - ○ The chicks are on a branch.
   - ○ They have a quilt for the sheep.

5.
   - ○ Let's get them out of the puddle.
   - ○ Let's quit watching the whale.
   - ○ Let's chase them into the garden.

Harcourt

Say the name of the first picture in each row. Color the pictures whose names begin with the same sounds.

Initial Blends with *s* • Phonemic Awareness

Phonics Practice Book

Harcourt

Name _____

Say the name of each picture. Circle the letters that stand for the beginning sounds. Then write the letters on the lines.

1	(sl) / sp / sk	2	st / sc / sp	3	sk / sm / sp
sl					

4	st / sc / sm	5	sk / sl / sp	6	sn / sl / st

7	sk / sn / sp	8	sl / sm / sn	9	sn / sc / st

10	st / sn / sc	11	sp / st / sc	12	sk / sp / sl

Name _____

Say each picture name. Circle and write the letters that stand for the beginning sounds. Then trace the rest of the word.

1	sp ⟨st⟩ sm	2	sl sn sk	3	sn sl sc
	stop		ip		ap

4	st sk sp	5	sp sl sn	6	sn sm st
	amp		ip		all

7	st sp sn	8	sl st sn	9	sk sl st
	in		ack		ick

10	sc sl sp	11	sl sn st	12	sk sp st
	ot		ack		ill

Initial Blends with *s*

Phonics Practice Book

Harcourt

Name _____

Circle the sentence that tells about each picture.

1		Dan and Pam stand on the hill. Dan and Pam skip up the hill. Dan and Pam slid down the hill.
2		This hill is not small. This snack is too big. This stick will not snap!
3		Dan and Pam pick up stamps. Dan and Pam snap a stick. Dan and Pam stop for a snack.
4		He stands still. He spins a small top. He skids and spills it.
5		She stops the spill. She sits still. She stands in a stall.

Harcourt

cast Color each picture whose name ends with the sounds /st/.

 mask Color each picture whose name ends with the sounds /sk/.

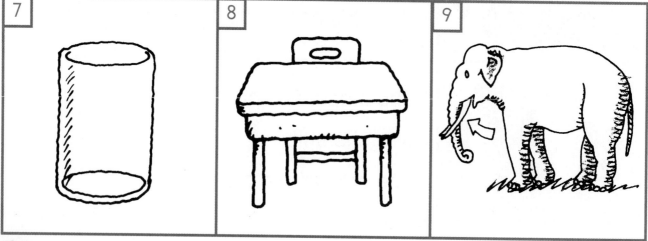

Name _____

Say the name of each picture. If the word ends with the sounds /st/, write **st** on the lines.

ca<u>st</u>

| 1 | 2 | 3 |

| 4 | 5 | 6 |

Say the name of each picture. If it ends with the sounds /sk/, write **sk** on the lines.

ma<u>sk</u>

| 7 | 8 | 9 |

Name _____

Say the name of the first picture in the row. Color each picture whose name begins with the same sounds.

1	ribbon	king	pie	pretzel	ring
2	truck	tent	tree	rope	train
3	drop	drum	rug	deer	dress
4	frame	fish	frog	fruit	tree
5	gravy boat	grass	rake	grapes	goat
6	crab	cat	crown	brush	crib

Initial Blends with *r* • Phonemic Awareness

Phonics Practice Book

Harcourt

Name _____

Say each picture name. Write the two letters that stand for the beginning sounds.

| cr | dr | fr | gr | pr | tr |

1	2	3
tr		

4	5	6

7	8	9

10	11	12

Harcourt

Name _____

Say each picture name. Circle and write the letters that stand for the beginning sounds. Then trace the rest of the word.

1	fr (gr) tr	grin
2	dr cr pr	op
3	fr cr tr	ack

4	gr fr tr	ill
5	dr gr tr	ip
6	dr fr tr	ink

7	pr fr cr	og
8	dr pr cr	ill
9	gr pr cr	ack

Harcourt

114   Initial Blends with *r*

Phonics Practice Book

Name _____

Look at each picture. Circle the word that completes the sentence. Then write the word.

1	Fran and Tramp go to the _____ ---------- _____.	track stack tack
2	Tramp sees a big _____ ---------- _____.	crack cap drink
3	Tramp is on the _____ ---------- _____.	grab grass drill
4	Fran sees a _____ ---------- _____.	crop prop drop
5	Now she sees a _____ ---------- _____.	grill rock frog

REVIEW

Say each picture name. Write the two letters that stand for the beginning sounds.

st	sc	sm	sp	sn	sl
tr	cr	pr	dr	gr	fr

Write the two letters that stand for the beginning or ending sounds.

st   sk

Phonics Practice Book

Harcourt

Name _____

Write the word that names each picture. Use two letters from the box to begin each word.

st	sc	sm	sp	sn	sl	sk
tr	cr	pr	dr	gr	fr	

1. _____

2. _____

3. _____

4. _____

5. _____

6. _____

7. _____

8. _____

Harcourt

Name _____

Say the name of the first picture in the row. Color the pictures whose names begin with the same sounds.

Initial Blends with /

Phonics Practice Book

Write the two letters that complete each picture name.
Then trace the rest of the word.

cl   fl   pl

1

_____
- - - - - - - - - -
ap
_____

2

_____
- - - - - - - - - -
ag
_____

3

_____
- - - - - - - - - -
ant
_____

4

_____
- - - - - - - - - -
ock
_____

5

_____
- - - - - - - - - -
ip
_____

6

_____
- - - - - - - - - -
am
_____

Harcourt

Name _____

Write the letters that complete each picture name. Then trace the whole word.

1 _____ _ _ _ _ ne	2 _____ _ _ _ _ am	3 _____ _ _ _ _ og
4 _____ _ _ _ _ all	5 _____ _ _ _ _ op	6 _____ _ _ _ _ in
7 _____ _ _ _ _ de	8 _____ _ _ _ _ amp	9 _____ _ _ _ _ ag
10 _____ _ _ _ _ ack	11 _____ _ _ _ _ unk	12 _____ _ _ _ _ ed

Cumulative Review of Consonant Blends

Phonics Practice Book

Harcourt

Name _____

Look at each picture. Circle the word that completes the sentence. Then write the word.

1	_____ The _____ hops.	drag frog flop
2	_____ Now he _____ .	swims trims spins
3	He stops for a _____ _____ .	track stack snack
4	Come and play in the _____ _____ .	glass grass class
5	_____ I can still do a _____ .	trip drip flip
6	_____ You need _____ to do this trick!	spill skill still

Harcourt

Name _____

CHECK-UP

Fill in the circle next to the word that names each picture.

1
- ○ vent
- ○ vest
- ○ vet

2
- ○ flap
- ○ slap
- ○ clap

3
- ○ grin
- ○ spin
- ○ drip

4
- ○ slick
- ○ click
- ○ stick

5
- ○ slip
- ○ skip
- ○ grip

6
- ○ drab
- ○ grab
- ○ crab

7
- ○ flock
- ○ clock
- ○ crock

8
- ○ skip
- ○ snip
- ○ clip

9
- ○ track
- ○ crack
- ○ stack

10
- ○ press
- ○ dress
- ○ fresh

11
- ○ skill
- ○ spill
- ○ still

12
- ○ plant
- ○ slant
- ○ grass

Consonant Blends Test   Phonics Practice Book

Name _____

Fill in the circle next to the sentence that tells about the picture.

1	○ We stand still.
	○ We are on a trip.
	○ We eat a snack.

2	○ They flip and do tricks.
	○ They rest in a nest.
	○ They smash a plant.

3	○ She grabs a small clam.
	○ She steps on a stick.
	○ She has spots on her skin.

4	○ They snap at a frog.
	○ They have wings that flap.
	○ They slip and fall in a crack.

5	○ He grips a fresh stem.
	○ He skips and is slim.
	○ He sniffs a good smell.

6	○ Let's fix this with a clip!
	○ Let's plan more trips like this!
	○ Let's stop and drop this drill!

Harcourt

Name _____

Say the name of the first picture in each row. Circle the picture whose name rhymes with it.

Short Vowel: / a / • Phonemic Awareness

Phonics Practice Book

Name _____

Say the names of the pictures in each row. Color the pictures whose names rhyme.

1.

2.

3.

4.

5.

Short Vowel: / a / • Phonemic Awareness

Color the pictures whose names have the vowel sound
/ a /.

Short Vowel: / a / • Phonemic Awareness

Phonics Practice Book

Harcourt

Name _____

Help the 🐱 get to the ▬. Color the pictures whose names have the vowel sound /a/.

Short Vowel: / a / • Phonemic Awareness

Name _____

Draw two things that rhyme with .

Short Vowel: / a / • Phonemic Awareness

Phonics Practice Book

Harcourt

Name _____

c<u>a</u>t

Write **a** under each word that has the vowel sound /a/.

1	2	3
a		

4	5	6

7	8	9

10	11	12

Harcourt

pat

Write four words that rhyme with **pat.** Then color the pictures.

1	2

_____

sat

_____

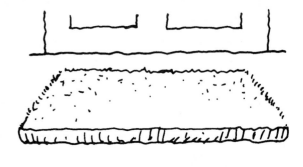

_____

- - - - - - - - - - - - - -

_____

3	4

_____

- - - - - - - - - - - - - -

_____

_____

- - - - - - - - - - - - - -

_____

Short Vowel: / a / a • Phonograms

Phonics Practice Book

Harcourt

Name _____

tap

Write two words that rhyme with **tap.** Then color the pictures.

1

_____

t a p

2

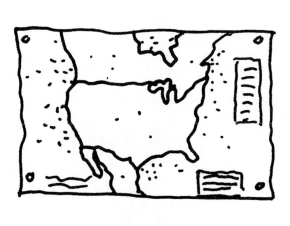

_____

3

_____

Harcourt

Name _____

Write the word that names each picture.

cap   ham   map   cat   tap   mat

1

_____
cap
_____

2

_____
_____
_____

3
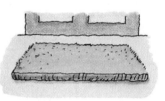
_____
_____
_____

4

_____
_____
_____

5
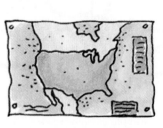
_____
_____
_____

6

_____
_____
_____

Short Vowel: / a / a • Reading Words with Short a

Phonics Practice Book

Name _____

Circle the word that completes each sentence.
Then write the word.

1		I am a _____.	cap cat
2		Here is a _____.	map hat
3		The cat _____.	sat taps
4		Here is a _____.	pat mat
5		Look at _____ that _____!	ham cap

Name _____

Say the name of the first picture in each row. Circle the picture whose name rhymes with it.

1			

2			

3			

4			

5			

Short Vowel: / i / • Phonemic Awareness

Phonics Practice Book

Harcourt

Say the names of the pictures in each row. Color the pictures whose names rhyme.

1

2

3

4

5

Short Vowel: / i / • Phonemic Awareness

Harcourt

Name _____

Circle and color the pictures whose names have the vowel sound /i/.

Short Vowel: / i / i • Phonemic Awareness

Phonics Practice Book

Harcourt

Name _____

pig

Write **i** under each picture whose name has the vowel sound /i/.

1	2	3
i		

4	5	6

7	8	9

10	11	12

Name _____

Say the name of each picture. Write the word in the boxes. Each new word will have two letters from the word before it.

1	d	i	p
2			
3			
4			
5			

Short Vowel: / i / *i*

Harcourt

Name _____

The picture names in each row rhyme. Write the rhyming words.

1 |

pit
_____ _____

2

dip
_____ _____

Harcourt

Slide and read each word. Color the picture it names.

1	p i t	
2	s i p	
3	s i t	
4	h i t	
5	h i d	

Short Vowel: / i / i • Blending

Phonics Practice Book

Harcourt

Name _____

Write **i** to complete each word. Trace the rest of the word. Then draw a picture for the word.

1	2
_____ p t	_____ s t

3	4
_____ s p	_____ h t

5	6
_____ t p	_____ h d

Harcourt

Name _____

Look at each picture. Write the word that completes the sentence.

| hit | pit | sip | hid | tip | sit |

1		_____ Tim has a _____.
2		_____ This is a big _____.
3		_____ See Pam _____.
4		_____ Come and _____ here.
5		_____ See it _____!
6		_____ The dog _____.

Harcourt

Short Vowel: / i / i

Phonics Practice Book

Name _____

Circle the sentence that tells about each picture.

1		The dog has a hat. The big dog sits.
2		I did it! It is a map!
3		Look at the cats. Look at the pits.
4		Tim hid here. Tim is sad.
5		Did Sid pat it? Did Sid sip it?

Harcourt

Name _____

Write **a** or **i** to complete each picture name. Then trace the rest of the word.

1	2	3
s _ t	c _ t	s _ p

4	5	6
h _ m	p _ t	c _ p

7	8	9
h _ t	m _ t	t _ p

10	11	12
s _ d	d _ p	h _ d

144

Review of Short Vowels: *a, i*

Phonics Practice Book

Harcourt

Read the story. Write words from the story to complete the sentences.

This Cat

Look at this cat.

This cat sits on me.

I pat the cat.

It looks at the hat.

It hits the hat!

Look at this cat!

_____
- - - - - - - - - - - - - - - - - -

1. The cat _____ on me.

_____
- - - - - - - - - - - - - - - - -

2. I _____ the cat.

_____
- - - - - - - - - - - - - - - - -

3. The cat _____ the hat.

Harcourt

Say the names of the pictures in each row. Color the pictures whose names rhyme.

1.

2.

3.

4.

5.

Short Vowel: / o / • Phonemic Awareness

Phonics Practice Book

Harcourt

Name _____

Color the pictures whose names have the vowel sound /o/.

Name _____

pot

Write **o** to complete each picture name that has the vowel sound /o/. Then trace the rest of the word.

1 c o t	2 c ___ t	3 ___ t p
4 c ___ n	5 m ___ p	6 s ___ ck
7 h ___ p	8 d ___ ll	9 s ___ ck
10 h ___ t	11 p ___ n	12 l ___ ck

Short Vowel: / o / o

Phonics Practice Book

Harcourt

Write the name of each picture.

1 _____ sock _____	2 _____ ------------- _____
3 _____ ------------- _____	4 _____ ------------- _____
5 _____ ------------- _____	6 _____ ------------- _____

Name _____

1. | p | o | t |

2. | | | |

3. | | | |

4. | | | |

5. | | | |

Short Vowel: / o / o

Phonics Practice Book

Harcourt

Name _____

clock Write the picture names that rhyme with **clock**.

1	2

1

![clock]

———————————
c l o c k
———————————

2

———————————
- - - - - - - - - - - -
———————————

3

———————————
- - - - - - - - - - - -
———————————

4

———————————
- - - - - - - - - - - -
———————————

Harcourt

STOP

stop

Write the picture names that rhyme with **stop**.
Then add one more rhyming word and picture.

1

top

2

_____

_____

3

_____

4

_____

Short Vowel: / o / o • Phonograms

Phonics Practice Book

Harcourt

Slide and read each word. Color the picture it names.

1 h o t

2 t o p

3 c o t

4 m o p

5 p o t

Short Vowel: / o / o • Blending

Harcourt

Name _____

Look at each picture. Write the word from the box that completes the sentence.

| hot | lock | hop | top | lot | cot |

1
It can _____ .

2
Don has a _____ of pots.

3
It is too _____ .

4
Tom has a _____ .

5
A cat is on the _____ .

6
I will _____ it.

Harcourt

Name _____

Circle the sentence that tells about each pictu[re]

1		You can nod at me. You can hop in. You can see the mop.
2		See me hop. See my doll. See me on the cot.
3		I had a big dog. I see the sock. It is on top.
4		It has lots of dots! It is on the dock! It pops and pops!
5		I will hop on the cot. I will pick a big pot. I will pop the top.
6		It is in the pot. It is a big dot. It is not hot.

Harcourt

the pictures in each row. Color the
...nes rhyme.

Short Vowel: / e / • Phonemic Awareness

Phonics Practice Book

Name _____

Say the name of each picture. Color the pictures whose names have the vowel sound /e/.

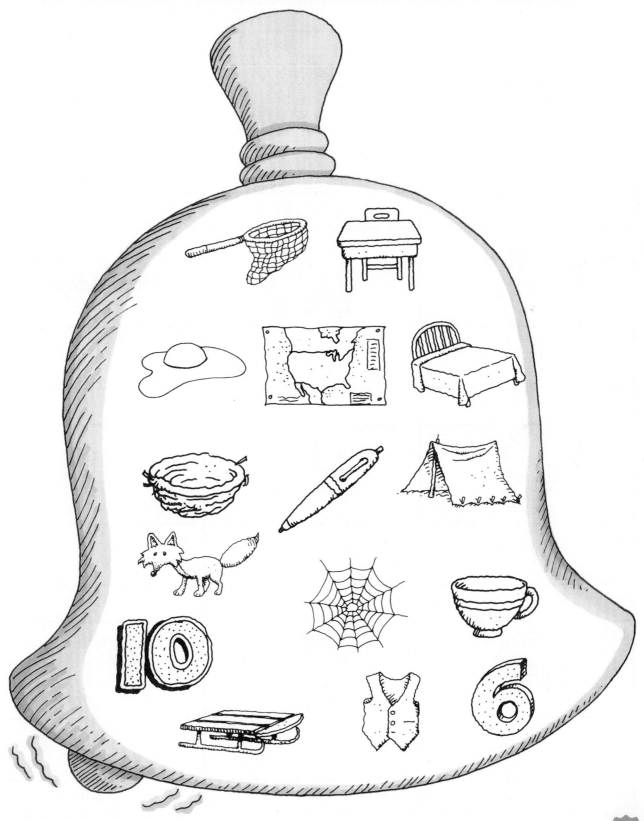

Harcourt

Short Vowel: / e / • Phonemic Awareness

bell

Write **e** to complete each picture name that has the vowel sound /e/. Then trace the rest of the word.

1	2	3
n ___ st	n ___ t	c ___ p
4	**5**	**6**
w ___ t	m ___ n	s l ___ d
7	**8**	**9**
h ___ n	f ___ sh	w ___ b
10	**11**	**12**
d ___ sk	s ___ ck	b ___ d

Name _____

Say the name of each picture. Write the word in the boxes. Each new word will have two letters from the word before it.

1. | l | o | g |

2. | | | |

3. | | | |

4. | | | |

5. | | | |

Short Vowel: / e / e

Write the name of each picture.

1	2	3
_____ vet _____	_____ _____	_____ _____
4	5	6
_____ _____	_____ _____	_____ _____
7	8	9
_____ _____	_____ _____	_____ _____

Short Vowel: / e / e • Writing Words with Short e

Phonics Practice Book

Harcourt

Name _____

The picture names in each row rhyme. Write the rhyming words.

1

v<u>et</u>

_____ _____

2

p<u>en</u>

_____ _____

Slide and read each word. Color the picture it names.

1. **h e n**

2. **s e t**

3. **p e n**

4. **w e b**

5. **b e l l**

Short Vowel: / e / e • Blending

Phonics Practice Book

Harcourt

Name _____

Look at each picture. Write the word from the box that completes the sentence.

hen   met   wet   fed   men   get

1. _____

She will _____ in.

2. _____

She _____ the dog.

3. _____

The _____ will go in.

4. But she will be

_____

_____ .

5. _____

The _____
are not sad.

6. Sam has not

_____

_____ Ben.

Harcourt

Name _____

1	Ken will see the hen. Ken will not get wet. Ken walks with the men.
2	You will get well. You went on a sled. You need this red shell.
3	My pet is in a web. She rests on a bed. A bell is on her neck.
4	Get the hen out of the well. Set the pen down. Let Ben see the hen.
5	The hen will get wet. I bet Ed has a net. Tell me why you fell.
6	The pens are on a desk. The eggs are in a nest. The pets fell out of bed.

Name _____

Beth's Hens

Nell and Meg are Beth's pet hens. They sleep in a shed. Beth's hens like to get fed. Meg is the red one. She bends her neck and pecks.

Beth finds eggs in the nest. She will sell the eggs. But she will not sell her hens. They are the best!

1. What do the hens like?

_____

- -

_____

2. What does Beth find?

_____

- -

_____

3. Will Beth sell her hens? Write why or why not.

_____

- -

_____

Harcourt

Name _____

Write **o** or **e** to complete each picture name. Then trace the rest of the word.

1	2	3	4
b d	m p	p t	h n

5	6	7	8
t p	n t	h n	n ck

9	10	11	12
c t	h p	b ll	w b

Review of Short Vowels: / o / o, / e / e

Phonics Practice Book

Harcourt

Name _____

 REVIEW

A frog is on the desk.

A nest is on a log.

A doll is on the bed.

Meg shops for socks.

Her dress has red dots.

Meg got a mop.

Ken went to the top.

Tom fell out of bed.

Don will get wet.

Where will the sled stop?

Why are the hens hot?

What has Fred got now?

Say the names of the pictures in each row. Color the pictures whose names rhyme.

1.

2.

3.

4.

5.

Short Vowel: / u / • Phonemic Awareness

Phonics Practice Book

Harcourt

Name _____

Say the name of each picture. Color the pictures whose names have the vowel sound /u/.

Short Vowel: / u / • Phonemic Awareness

Say the name of each picture. Write the word in the boxes. Each new word will have two letters from the word before it.

1 | c | a | t |

2 | | | |

3 | | | |

4 | | | |

5 | | | |

Short Vowel: / u / u   •   Writing Words with Short u

Phonics Practice Book

Harcourt

Name _____

Write the name of each picture.

1	2	3
nut		

4	5	6

7	8	9

Name _____

The picture names in each row rhyme. Write the rhyming words.

1

f**un**

_____
- - - - - - - - - - - - - - - -
_____

_____
- - - - - - - - - - - - - - - -
_____

2

s**um**

_____
- - - - - - - - - - - - - - - -
_____

_____
- - - - - - - - - - - - - - - -
_____

3

t**ub**

_____
- - - - - - - - - - - - - - - -
_____

_____
- - - - - - - - - - - - - - - -
_____

Short Vowel: / u / u • Phonograms

Phonics Practice Book

Name _____

Slide and read each word. Color the picture it names.

1 s u n

2 b u s

3 c u p

4 h u g

5 d r u m

Harcourt

Phonics Practice Book

Short Vowel: / u / *u* • Blending

173

Name _____

1	2	3
p __ p	b __ s	s __ n

4	5	6
b __ g	d __ ck	c __ b

7	8	9
dr __ m	s __ b	tr __ ck

Short Vowel: / u / u • Reading Words with Short u

Phonics Practice Book

Name _____

Look at each picture. Write the word from the box that completes the sentence.

rug	mud	tug
bus	bun	fun

1. The hot dog comes on a _____ _____.

2. We can't play in the _____.

3. So we play on the _____.

4. We all have to _____!

5. We can always have _____.

6. We get on the _____.

Short Vowel: / u / u • Reading Words with Short u

Harcourt

Name _____

Read the story. Write words from the story to complete the sentences.

ON THE BUS

Bud the bug got on the bus. The ducks said, "Bud must sit with us." Then the skunks and the cubs got into a fuss. "It's more fun up here with us!"

When the bus got stuck in the mud, that was the end of the fuss over Bud.

_____
- -

1. Bud got on _____.

_____   _____
- - - - - - - - - - - - - - - - -   - - - - - - - - - - - - - - - -

2. The _____ and the _____
fussed over Bud.

_____
- -

3. The bus got _____

_____
- -
_____.

Short Vowel: / u / u • Reading Words in Context   Phonics Practice Book

Name _____

Do what the sentences tell you.

1. Do you see the sun? Color it.

2. Look for the truck. Color it red.

3. Now find the bus. Color it, too.

4. Color the duck with the drum.

5. Put a bug on the cup.

6. Color the pup that tugs.

Now circle the words that have the vowel sound /u/.

Harcourt

Name _____

Write **a, e, i, o**, or **u** to complete each picture name.
Then trace the rest of the word.

1 b __ d	2 p __ t	3 h __ t
4 p __ g	5 b __ s	6 m __ p
7 t __ n	8 m __ p	9 f __ n
10 h __ ll	11 r __ g	12 n __ t

Cumulative Review of Short Vowels

Phonics Practice Book

Harcourt

Name _____

Circle the sentence that tells about each picture.

1
Dan will get the net.

Bill can fit in the bus.

Tom can hop and run.

2
Kim picks up the cup.

Dot hit it with the bat.

Pam sat on the hill.

3
This pig will fix the fan.

The pig digs in the mud.

A pig gets wet in the well.

4
The fox sees ten big hens.

The duck sits with the bug.

The fox will not get in the bag.

5
The cub naps in his bed.

The bed is on a red rug.

The cub runs to the top.

Harcourt

Name _____

Fill in the circle next to the name of each picture.

1
- ○ hat
- ○ hot
- ○ hut

2
- ○ pan
- ○ pond
- ○ pin

3
- ○ cab
- ○ cub
- ○ cob

4
- ○ pet
- ○ pit
- ○ pot

5
- ○ nut
- ○ not
- ○ net

6
- ○ big
- ○ bug
- ○ bag

7
- ○ sack
- ○ sock
- ○ sick

8
- ○ hit
- ○ hot
- ○ hat

9
- ○ tin
- ○ ten
- ○ tan

10
- ○ cut
- ○ cot
- ○ cat

11
- ○ deck
- ○ dock
- ○ duck

12
- ○ bed
- ○ bad
- ○ bud

Fill in the circle next to the sentence that tells about the picture.

1		○ She likes her cap. ○ She picks up a cup. ○ She is in her bed.
2		○ The pot will get hot. ○ The rug is red and tan. ○ The can is not in the bag.
3		○ Let's mop up this mess. ○ Let's mix this in a pan. ○ Let's fill this big box.
4		○ Dad will fix the fan. ○ Tim has a big hat. ○ Bob cuts the grass.
5		○ A pig went up a hill. ○ A hen sits on a rock. ○ A fox hops in a tub.
6		○ Six cubs fit in the bed. ○ The dog and pups got wet. ○ Fat cats nap in the sun.

Harcourt

Name _____

Write **ea** under each picture whose name has the vowel sound /e/. Then trace the rest of the word.

1
br___d

2
t___ck

3
h___d

4
thr___d

5
f___sh

6
h___vy

Harcourt

Name _____

Look at each picture. Circle the word that completes the sentence. Then write the word.

1	Put this on your _____ .... _____ .	hill head had
2	_____ .... _____ , set, go!	Rock Ready Rip
3	We are out of _____ .... _____ .	brand bring breath
4	Here is the _____ .... _____ .	bread brick brag
5	_____ .... I will _____ it for you.	spot spring spread

Harcourt

Say the names of the pictures in each row. Color the pictures whose names rhyme.

1

2

3

4

5

Long Vowel: / ō / • Phonemic Awareness

Phonics Practice Book

Harcourt

Name _____

Help the  go over the . Color the pictures
whose names have the vowel sound /ō/.

Harcourt

Name _____

The picture names in each row rhyme. Write the rhyming words.

1

b<u>oa</u>t

_____

- - - - - - - - - - - - - - -

_____

_____

- - - - - - - - - - - - - - -

_____

2

sn<u>ow</u>

_____

- - - - - - - - - - - - - - -

_____

_____

- - - - - - - - - - - - - - -

_____

3

l<u>oa</u>d

_____

- - - - - - - - - - - - - - -

_____

_____

- - - - - - - - - - - - - - -

_____

Long Vowel: / ō / *ow, oa* • Phonograms   Phonics Practice Book

Slide and read each word. Color the picture it names.

1 b o a t	
2 s o a p	
3 c o a t	
4 b o w l	
5 t o a d	

Harcourt

Name _____

boat

Boat has the long **o** sound. Write **oa** to complete each word that has the sound /ō/. Then trace the rest of the word.

1	2	3
c_o_a_t	s___ _ p	___ c ___ t

4	5	6
___ t _ d	b ___ x	___ g ___ t

bow

Bow has the long **o** sound. Write **ow** to complete each word that has the sound /ō/. Then trace the rest of the word.

7	8	9
s n ___	p ___ t	b ___ l

Harcourt

Name ____________________

Circle the name of each picture. Then write the word.

1

got

get

goat

goat

2

mow

man

mop

3

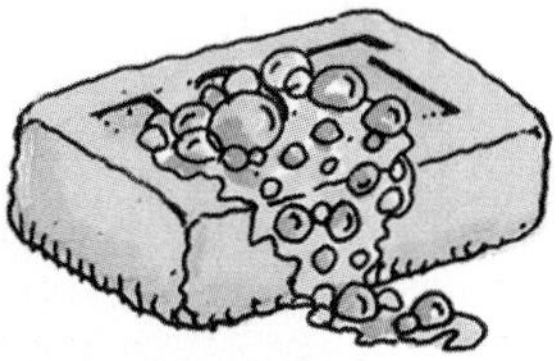

sop

soap

sip

4

bell

box

bowl

5

cat

coat

cot

6

lad

load

log

7

rod

road

rose

8

snap

snow

sock

9

bet

bat

boat

Name _____

Write the word that completes each sentence.

> **load**   **boat**   **slow**   **road**   **blow**

1. Cars and trucks are on the _____.

2. The dump truck has a big _____ of rocks.

3. One car has a _____.

4. They all are too _____.

5. Don't _____ your horn!

Harcourt

Name _____

Circle the word that completes each sentence. Then write the word.

1		_____ - _____ us what you got from Joan.	Show She Shop
2		Do you think they will _____ - - - - - - - - - - - - - - - - - - _____ in the dark?	glass glow glad
3		_____ - What a big _____!	bow bee boat
4		_____ - - - - - - - - - - - - - - - - - - Can he _____them all out?	block blend blow
5		I would like some in my _____ - _____.	back barn bowl
6		How much did _____ - - - - - - - - - - - - - - - - - - you _____?	grand grow grin

Harcourt

Name _____

Say the names of the pictures in each row. Color the pictures whose names rhyme.

Long Vowel: / ē / • Phonemic Awareness

Phonics Practice Book

Help the 🐑 get to the 🌳. Color the pictures whose names have the vowel sound /ē/.

Name _____

The picture names in each row rhyme. Write the rhyming words.

1

_____   _____

- - - - - - - - - - - - - - -   - - - - - - - - - - - - - - -

st<u>ea</u>m   _____   _____

2

_____   _____

- - - - - - - - - - - - - - -   - - - - - - - - - - - - - - -

sh<u>ee</u>p   _____   _____

3

_____   _____

- - - - - - - - - - - - - - -   - - - - - - - - - - - - - - -

thr<u>ee</u>   _____   _____

Long Vowel: / ē / e, ea, ee • Phonograms

Phonics Practice Book

Name _____

The **ea** in **bead**, the **ee** in **peel**, and the **e** in **me** all stand for the sound /ē/. Write the words where they belong in the lists. Then draw a picture for the last word in each list.

he	leaf	tree	beach	she
feet	dream	bee		we

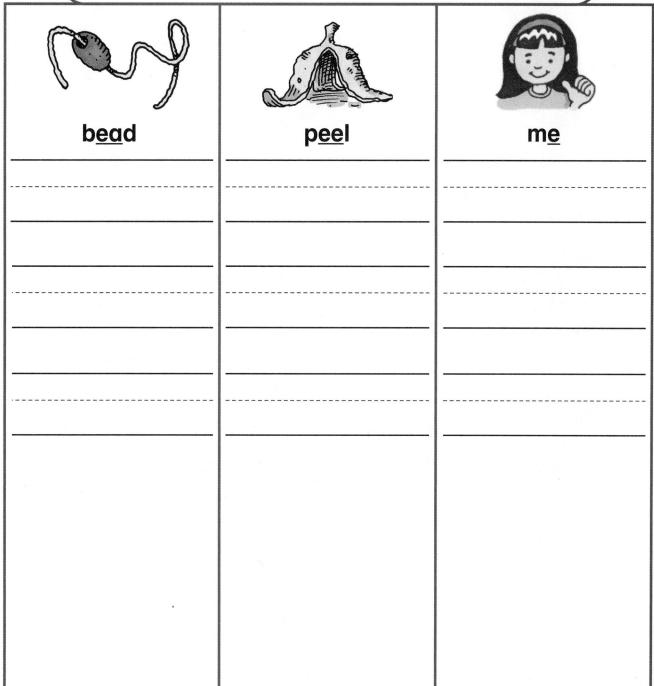

bead

peel

me

Harcourt

Slide and read each word. Color the picture it names.

1 **p e e l**

2 **l e a f**

3 **f e e t**

4 **t e a m**

5 **s e a l**

Long Vowel: / ē / e, ea, ee • Blending

Phonics Practice Book

Harcourt

Name _____

Circle the name of each picture. Then write the word.

1		2		3	
	bed		seed		beak
	boat		sell		best
	(bead)		sad		back
bead					

4		5		6	
	pill		hen		meal
	pet		he		melt
	peel		had		me

7		8		9	
	shed		fast		road
	sheep		felt		read
	ship		feet		rest

Name _____

| tree | eat | seed | beak | be | feed |

_____
- -

1. What does she have in her _____?

_____
- -

2. It is a big _____.

_____
- -

3. She takes it back to the _____.

_____
- -

4. She will _____ it there.

_____
- -

5. She will fly again to _____ her little ones.

_____
- -

6. They will _____ happy.

Long Vowel: / ē / e, ea, ee • Reading Words with Long e   Phonics Practice Book

Harcourt

Name _____

Read the story. Then answer the question.

A DAY AT THE BEACH

One day we went to the beach. We saw that the beach was not clean. We all put the trash in green bags.

We had our meal under a big tree. Jean shouted that she saw a seal. Lee saw three bees.

Then it was time to go. But first we needed to make the beach clean and neat. Next week we will come back to this beach by the sea.

Why did they clean the beach?

_____

- -

_____

_____

- -

_____

Harcourt

Name _____

Say the names of the pictures in each row. Color the pictures whose names rhyme.

1.

2.

3.

4.

5.

Long Vowel: /ā/ • Phonemic Awareness

Phonics Practice Book

Harcourt

Name _____

The picture names in each row rhyme. Write the rhyming words.

1

skate

_____   _____

- - - - - - - - - - - - - -   - - - - - - - - - - - - - -

_____   _____

2

snake

_____   _____

- - - - - - - - - - - - - -   - - - - - - - - - - - - - -

_____   _____

3

wave

_____   _____

- - - - - - - - - - - - - -   - - - - - - - - - - - - - -

_____   _____

Gate has the long **a** sound. Write **a** in the middle and **e** at the end of each word that has the sound /ā/. Then trace the rest of the word.

g<u>a</u>t<u>e</u>

1. w v	2. t p	3. c t
4. c n	5. sn k	6. g m
7. f l g	8. r k	9. sk t
10. c n	11. b g	12. c k

Harcourt

Slide and read each word. Color the picture it names.

1	c a k e			
2	t a p e			
3	c a n e			
4	s k a t e			
5	g a m e			

Harcourt

Name _____

1		2		3	
	rag rack (rake)		gate gape got		shave shack ship
rake					

4		5		6	
	can cane coat		tape tap top		goat gas game

7		8		9	
	grape grab grow		snack sneak snake		plane plate plot

Long Vowel: /ā/ *a-e* • Reading Words with Long *a*

Phonics Practice Book

Harcourt

Name _____

Circle the sentence that tells about each picture.

1 	We put on capes. We can't skate. We are on a plane.
2 	We like to wade in the lake. We like to bake a cake. We like the same game.
3 	Jake adds his name. Jake waves to Kate. Jake shakes a cane.
4 	Kate reads a tale. Kate came in the gate. Kate gave Jake a frame.
5 	Jake is late for the game. Kate made a snake shape. Kate and Jake take some tape.
6	Kate and Jake ate cake. The grapes are on a plate. The plate is in a cave.

Harcourt

Name _____

puppy

pupp<u>ie</u>s

The **y** in **puppy** and the **ie** in **puppies** both stand for the sound /ē/. Write the word that completes each sentence.

field　　sunny　　bunny　　happy　　bunnies

_____

1. Billy the _____ looked outside.

_____

2. It was _____ out.

_____

3. He got all the other _____.

_____

4. Now they are in the _____.

_____

5. They are _____ bunnies.

Long Vowel: / ē / y, ie　•　Reading Words with Long e

Phonics Practice Book

Harcourt

...e name of each picture. Then write the word.

1	happen happy hopping	2	field filled felt	3	puppets pumps puppies

4	supper sudden sunny	5	snort sneak snowy	6	pens ponds pennies

7	chief chain chill	8	mutter muddy muddle	9	chilly chicks chuckle

Name _____

Say the names of the pictures in each row. Color the pictures whose names rhyme.

1.

2.

3.

4.

5.

Long Vowel: /ī/ • Phonemic Awareness

Phonics Practice Book

Harcourt

The picture names in each row rhyme. Write the rhyming words.

1

hive

_____

- - - - - - - - - - -

_____

2

pine

_____

- - - - - - - - - - -

_____

3

slide

_____

- - - - - - - - - - -

_____

Harcourt

Nine has the long **i** sound. Write **i** in the middle and **e** at the end of each word that has the sound /ī/. Then trace the rest of the word.

n<u>i</u>n<u>e</u>

1 nine	2 r k	3 h v
4 p n	5 v n	6 d v
7 k t	8 b k	9 g m
10 h t	11 f v	12 l n

Harcourt

Slide and read each word. Color the picture it names.

1	k i t e		
2	p i n e		
3	r i d e		
4	b i k e		
5	v i n e		

Harcourt

Name _____

1.
buck
back
(bike)

bike

2.
hive
hit
hiss

_____

3.
pin
pine
pig

_____

4.
kick
kiss
kite

_____

5.
slide
slip
sleep

_____

6.
dig
dive
dish

_____

7.
lid
line
lane

_____

8.
bet
boat
bite

_____

9.
ride
rid
read

_____

Long Vowel: /ī/ *i-e* • Writing Words with Long *i*

Phonics Practice Book

Harcourt

Name _____

1. Mr. Miles rides a bike. Make a box around Mr. Miles.

2. What is a mile up? Color it.

3. Do you see a kite? Make it the same color as the vine.

4. Find the pile. Add one to make nine.

5. Swipe the cat likes to hide. Make a line
   under Swipe.

6. Put another cat by Swipe's side. This cat has stripes.

Now circle the words that have the sound /ī/.

Harcourt

Name _____

Say the names of the pictures in each row. Color the pictures whose names rhyme.

1

2

3

4

Long Vowel: /ī/ • Phonemic Awareness

Phonics Practice Book

Harcourt

Name _____

shy

lie

The **y** in **shy** and the **ie** in **lie** both stand for the long **i** sound. Write the word that completes each sentence.

| tie | fly | pie | try | sky |

_____

1. Birds can _____.

_____

2. They go up in the _____.

_____

3. I'll _____ these wings to my shell.

_____

4. Then I'll give it a _____.

_____

5. Oh my! Don't cry. Have some _____.

Long Vowel: /ī/ y, ie • Reading Words with Long *i*

Harcourt

Name _____

Say the names of the pictures in each row. Color the pictures whose names rhyme.

1

2

3

4

5

Long Vowel: / ō / • Phonemic Awareness

Phonics Practice Book

Harcourt

Name _____

The picture names in each row rhyme. Write the rhyming words.

1

mole

2

hose

3

stone

Harcourt

Name _____

rope

Rope has the long **o** sound. Write **o** in the middle and **e** at the end of each word that has the sound /ō/. Then trace the rest of the word.

1	2	3
r p	b n	m p

4	5	6
p l	p t	r s

7	8	9
t p	r b	c n

10	11	12
n s	b x	h l

218   Long Vowel: / ō / o-e

Phonics Practice Book

Harcourt

Slide and read each word. Color the picture it names.

1	p o l e			
2	r o b e			
3	s m o k e	STOP		
4	h o s e			
5	c o n e			

Long Vowel: / ō / o-e • Blending

Harcourt

Name _____

1. nod
    nest
    (nose)

    nose

2. rope
    rock
    row

3. meal
    mole
    mop

4. not
    net
    note

5. can
    cone
    cane

6. rob
    robe
    rub

7. rods
    road
    rose

8. pal
    pole
    pill

9. bean
    bun
    bone

Harcourt

Name _____

Write the word that completes each sentence.

hose	bone	joke
mole	hope	hole

_____

1. I have a big _____ .

_____

2. I will put it in this _____ .

_____

3. Joan went to get the _____ .

_____

4. I _____ she does not see me.

_____

5. I'll say a _____ did it.

_____

6. Will she laugh at my _____ ?

Harcourt

Name _____

Write the word that names each picture.

kite	pie	bow	team	rope	cake
field	dry	me	happy	bee	boat

1

_____

- - - - - - - - - - - - - - -

_____

2

_____

- - - - - - - - - - - - - - -

_____

3

_____

- - - - - - - - - - - - - - -

_____

4

_____

- - - - - - - - - - - - - - -

_____

5

_____

- - - - - - - - - - - - - - -

_____

6

_____

- - - - - - - - - - - - - - -

_____

7

_____

- - - - - - - - - - - - - - -

_____

8

_____

- - - - - - - - - - - - - - -

_____

9

_____

- - - - - - - - - - - - - - -

_____

10

_____

- - - - - - - - - - - - - - -

_____

11

_____

- - - - - - - - - - - - - - -

_____

12

_____

- - - - - - - - - - - - - - -

_____

Review of Long Vowels: /ō/, /ē/, /ā/, /ī/

Phonics Practice Book

Harcourt

Name _____

Circle and write the word that completes each sentence.

1	_____ - - - - - - - - - - - - - - - This is the _____ to take.	read road ride
2	_____ - - - - - - - - - - - - - - - Mr. Lee lives a _____ up the hill.	mile mole meal
3	_____ - - - - - - - - - - - - - - - He _____ when he sees us.	waves weeps wipes
4	You can see the lights _____ - - - - - - - - - - - - - - - _____ .	glee glow glide
5	Debbie gave the puppy a _____ - - - - - - - - - - - - - - - _____ .	by bean bone
6	_____ - - - - - - - - - - - - - - - We feel _____ at Mr. Lee's home.	heap happy heel

Harcourt

Name _____

right

The **igh** in **right** stands for the long **i** sound. Write the word that completes each sentence.

(light   high   night   fright   bright)

_____

1. One _____ I woke up.

2. I saw a _____ in the sky.

3. The light was very _____.

4. It gave me a _____.

5. It was a plane _____ up in the sky!

Name _____

1		2		3	
	sip sea (sigh)		light list lie		frog fright fry
	sigh				

4		5		6	
	bring bite bright		high hug hide		tag tight tie

7		8		9	
	ring right ride		nine nest night		flight flip float

Harcourt

Say the names of the pictures in each row. Color the pictures whose names rhyme.

1

2

3

4

5

Long Vowel: /ā/ • Phonemic Awareness

Phonics Practice Book

Harcourt

Name _____

Help the  get out of the ⫽ . Color the pictures whose names have the vowel sound /ā/.

Long Vowel: /ā/ • Phonemic Awareness

Harcourt

Name _____

The picture names in each row rhyme. Write the rhyming words.

1

_____   _____

- - - - - - - - - - - - - - -   - - - - - - - - - - - - - - -

m<u>ail</u>   _____   _____

2

_____   _____

- - - - - - - - - - - - - - -   - - - - - - - - - - - - - - -

ch<u>ain</u>   _____   _____

3

_____   _____

- - - - - - - - - - - - - - -   - - - - - - - - - - - - - - -

j<u>ay</u>   _____   _____

Long Vowel: /ā/ *ai, ay* • Phonograms   Phonics Practice Book

Harcourt

Name _____

Slide and read each word. Color the picture it names.

1. h a y

2. t a i l

3. t r a y

4. p a i l

5. r a i n

Long Vowel: / ā / *ai, ay* • Blending

Harcourt

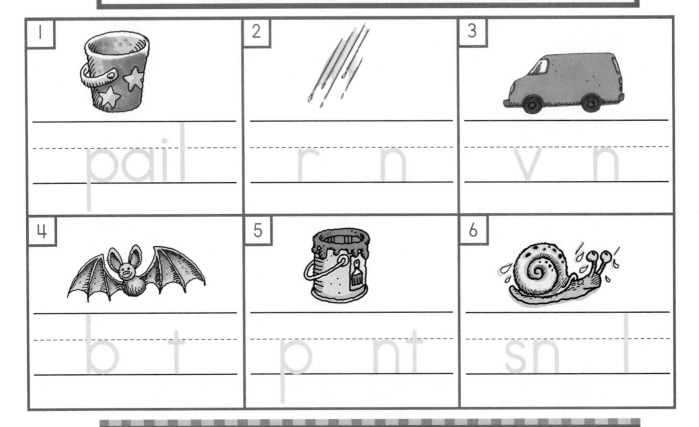

Mail has the long **a** sound. Write **ai** to complete each word that has the sound /ā/. Then trace the rest of the word.

m**ai**l

1	2	3
p<u>ai</u>l	r n	v n

4	5	6
b t	p nt	sn l

Jay has the long **a** sound. Write **ay** to complete each word that has the sound /ā/. Then trace the rest of the word.

j**ay**

7	8	9
d	pl	p n

Harcourt

Name _____

Circle the name of each picture. Then write the word.

1	pan pole (pail)
pail	

2	chain chin chart

3	hay hat how

4	jam jay jar

5	braid branch brick

6	rang ran rain

7	mail mile meal

8	trap trick train

9	soap say see

Harcourt

Name _____

Circle the sentence that tells about the picture.

1		This is the day to play with Kay. This is the way to Main Street. This is the mail for Ray Green.
2		Gail has a braid. Gail has a pain. Gail has some clay.
3		Ray stays away. Ray waits all day. Ray pays for the nails.
4		The snail makes a trail. The pail may sail away. The chain is on a train.
5		Let's pay for this tray. Let's play in this hay. Let's paint this gray.
6		He may bring in the mail! He got paint on his tail! He put grain in his pail!

Long Vowel: / ā / ai, ay

Phonics Practice Book

Harcourt

Name _____

Do what the sentences tell you. Then circle the words that have the sound /ā/.

1. Give the painter a pail of paint.

2. Find the tray.  Color the plain cake on the tray.

3. Kay has braids and likes to play. Write **Kay** next to her.

4. Mrs. Day brings the mail. Write **Mrs. Day** next to her.

5. Jay has a boat. Put a sail on it.

6. Find the gray dog that waits. Put a tail on him.

Harcourt

Name _____

The **i** in **hi** stands for the sound /ī/. Write the word that completes each sentence.

hi

find   child   I   grind   kind

_____

1. Who will help me _____ this wheat?

_____ "

2. "Not _____, said the pig.

_____

3. Can the hen _____ some help?

_____

4. A _____ helps the hen.

_____ "

5. "You are very _____, says the hen.

Harcourt

Name _____

Write the word that completes each sentence.

find　　I　　wild　　kind　　behind

1		My cat Spike _____ ---------------------------------- is a little bit _____.
2		He likes to hide _____ ---------------------------------- _____ things.
3		Other cats always _____ ---------------------------------- _____ him!
4		_____ ---------------------------------- One time, _____ saw that Spike was sick.
5		The vet was _____ ---------------------------------- very _____ to him.

Name _____

Old has the sound /ō/. Write **o** to complete each word that has the sound /ō/. Then trace the rest of the word.

old

1.
old

2.
pple

3.
c ld

4.
n

5.
f ld

6.
f x

7.
k te

8.
s ld

9.
g ld

Long Vowel: / ō / o

Phonics Practice Book

Harcourt

Name _____

Circle and write the word that completes each sentence.

#			
1		_____ Can we _____ for a swim?	got go game
2		_____ I will _____ mine.	feed fog fold
3		_____ I like to _____ it up.	roll rock rail
4		_____ The water is _____.	cot cake cold
5		_____ Now _____ of us are warm!	box both bay

Name _____

Find the words in the puzzle. Circle them. Some words go across. Some words go down.

mule   cute   huge   cube

c	u	b	e	m
u	l	r	w	h
t	f	s	o	u
e	d	t	k	g
z	m	u	l	e

Now write the word that names each picture.

1.
_____
- - - - - - - - - - - - - - - - -
_____

2.
_____
- - - - - - - - - - - - - - - - -
_____

3.
_____
- - - - - - - - - - - - - - - - -
_____

4.
_____
- - - - - - - - - - - - - - - - -
_____

Long Vowel: / (y)o͞o / u-e

Phonics Practice Book

Name _____

Write the word that completes each sentence.

huge   use   cute
mule   cube

_____
----

1. The _____ is in the flowers.

_____
----

2. The boy will _____ his cap to chase it out.

_____
----

3. The baby ducks are _____.

_____
----

4. That baby duck thinks the horse is _____.

_____
----

5. Mother puts an ice _____ in the water.

Name _____

| mule | light | find | night | rain | gold | cube | tray | mail |

1

_____

- - - - - - - - - - - - - - - - - - - -

_____

2

_____

- - - - - - - - - - - - - - - - - - - -

_____

3

_____

- - - - - - - - - - - - - - - - - - - -

_____

4

_____

- - - - - - - - - - - - - - - - - - - -

_____

5

_____

- - - - - - - - - - - - - - - - - - - -

_____

6

_____

- - - - - - - - - - - - - - - - - - - -

_____

7

_____

- - - - - - - - - - - - - - - - - - - -

_____

8

_____

- - - - - - - - - - - - - - - - - - - -

_____

9

_____

- - - - - - - - - - - - - - - - - - - -

_____

Harcourt

Name _____

1	What did you _____ ----------------------- _____?	find fold fill
2	_____ ----------------------- It's a _____ chain.	goat go gold
3	_____ ----------------------- It's so _____!	bring bright braid
4	I've looked all _____ ----------------------- _____ for this!	day dad dark
5	It plays a happy _____ ----------------------- _____.	tub tune tail

Harcourt

Name _____

Write the word that names each picture.

goat	cube	kite	cake	leaf	hay
train	bowl	tree	cone	pie	night

1

_____
- - - - - - - - - - -
_____

2

_____
- - - - - - - - - - -
_____

3

_____
- - - - - - - - - - -
_____

4

_____
- - - - - - - - - - -
_____

5

_____
- - - - - - - - - - -
_____

6

_____
- - - - - - - - - - -
_____

7

_____
- - - - - - - - - - -
_____

8

_____
- - - - - - - - - - -
_____

9

_____
- - - - - - - - - - -
_____

10

_____
- - - - - - - - - - -
_____

11

_____
- - - - - - - - - - -
_____

12

_____
- - - - - - - - - - -
_____

Harcourt

Cumulative Review of Long Vowels

Phonics Practice Book

Name _____

ACROSS THE SEA

One fine day Annie, Kenny, and Ray sailed out to sea. Their boat rolled over waves as they made their way east. They felt the sun's heat on their cheeks. Then the waves began to grow.

"Oh no!" shouted Kenny. "Our boat has a leak! Take a pail and start to bail while I try to find the hole." The hole was huge, but Kenny used pieces of a crate to plug it up tight. Then they sailed into a cove and rested. They were happy watching the whales and seals.

1. What happened to the boat when the waves got big?

----

2. What did Annie, Kenny, and Ray do about the leak?

Harcourt

Name _____

Fill in the circle next to the name of each picture.

1
- ○ sat
- ○ soap
- ○ sip

2
- ○ cub
- ○ cab
- ○ cube

3
- ○ bad
- ○ bed
- ○ bead

4
- ○ rope
- ○ rain
- ○ ran

5
- ○ tape
- ○ tap
- ○ top

6
- ○ bee
- ○ bay
- ○ bow

7
- ○ hat
- ○ hay
- ○ hold

8
- ○ note
- ○ net
- ○ night

9
- ○ sheep
- ○ show
- ○ shape

10
- ○ kick
- ○ kite
- ○ kit

11
- ○ robe
- ○ rob
- ○ rug

12
- ○ cot
- ○ cold
- ○ cane

Harcourt

Name _____

Fill in the circle next to the sentence that tells about each picture.

1	○ Dave shows her a goat. ○ Jake eats his meal. ○ Mike takes the mail.
2	○ A snake meets a snail. ○ A seal dreams of the sea. ○ A shy snail eats a pie.
3	○ The blue jay sees a kite. ○ A jay plays with a rope. ○ He has a seed in his beak.
4	○ The puppy eats ice cubes. ○ The puppy's bone floats away. ○ The puppy's nose is bright.
5	○ The mule uses a light at night. ○ The mule plays a tune in a field. ○ The mule will find green grapes.
6	○ Rose paints an old gate gray. ○ Joan uses soap on the sheep. ○ Kate makes a goat from clay.

Harcourt

Name _____

Underline the word that answers the question. Then write the word.

1		A can or a cane?	
2		A bed or a bead?	
3		A kit or a kite?	
4		A cot or a coat?	
5		A pad or paid?	
6		Ran or rain?	
7		A cub or a cube?	
8		A pin or a pine?	

Harcourt

Read each word. Add a vowel to make it a word with a long vowel sound. Draw a picture for each new word.

1	set	_____ ----------------- _____	
2	can	_____ ----------------- _____	
3	cut	_____ ----------------- _____	
4	got	_____ ----------------- _____	
5	pin	_____ ----------------- _____	
6	ran	_____ ----------------- _____	

Harcourt

Name _____

Read each clue. Find the answer in the box. Then write the word.

What Is It?

fish	skates
cone	sun
bike	sled

1	You ride it. It has two wheels.	_____
2	You can't use it on a hot day!	_____
3	You can feed it at the pond. It is not a duck.	_____
4	You go fast with these on your feet.	_____
5	Fill this with ice cream, and eat it!	_____
6	It shines brightly and makes you hot.	_____

Harcourt

Name _____

boat	snow
path	sled
pot	cold

What Is It?

1

It fell from the sky, but it is not rain.

_____

2

You need a snowy hill to use this.

_____

3

A man makes this clean so you can walk on it.

_____

4

You can't use this when there's ice on the pond.

_____

5

This will be a silly hat!

_____

6

This is how you'd feel without your coat.

_____

Harcourt

Name _____

Color each picture whose name has the vowel sound /ôr/.

R-controlled Vowel: / ôr / • Phonemic Awareness

Phonics Practice Book

Harcourt

Name _____

cork

Write **or** to complete each picture name that has the vowel sound /ôr/. Then trace the rest of the word.

1	2	3
horn	f___t	b___d

4	5	6
st___m	t___n	t___n

7	8	9
c___t	th___n	f___k

10	11	12
c___n	c___n	th
		g___t

Harcourt

Write the name of each picture.

1	2	3

4	5	6

7	8	9

R-controlled Vowel: / ôr / *or* • Writing Words

Phonics Practice Book

Harcourt

Name _____

horn

Write the picture names that rhyme with **horn**.
Then add one more rhyming word and picture.

1	2
horn	

3	4

Harcourt

Name _____

Slide and read each word. Color the picture it names.

1	c o r n	(can)	(corn)	(cot)
2	f o r k	(fork)	(fan)	5
3	s t o r m	(stamp)	(storm)	(stick)
4	h o r n	(hat)	(hand)	(horn)
5	f o r t	(fort)	(fish)	(fox)

R-controlled Vowel: / ôr / or • Blending   Phonics Practice Book

Harcourt

Name _____

Write **or** to complete each word. Then trace the rest of the word and draw a picture for the word.

1	2	3
c___n	f___k	th___n

4	5	6
f___t	st___m	h___n

Harcourt

Name _____

Write the word that completes each sentence.

corn   fort   torn   fork   storm   thorn

1		This is a big _____ .
2		This will be a good _____ .
3		Oh, it's a _____ !
4		Is it _____ ?
5		Put the _____ in a pan.
6		Put it on your _____ .

R-controlled Vowel: / ôr / or • Reading Words

Phonics Practice Book

Harcourt

Name _____

Read the rhyme. Write words from the rhyme to complete the sentences.

The dog plays a horn.
The cat got the corn.
The pig has a cork.
But where is the fork?
The stork has a hat.
Is there one for the cat?

1. The pig needs a _____ .

2. The cat has the _____ .

3. The _____ is the tall one.

Name _____

Say the names of the pictures in each row. Color the pictures whose names rhyme.

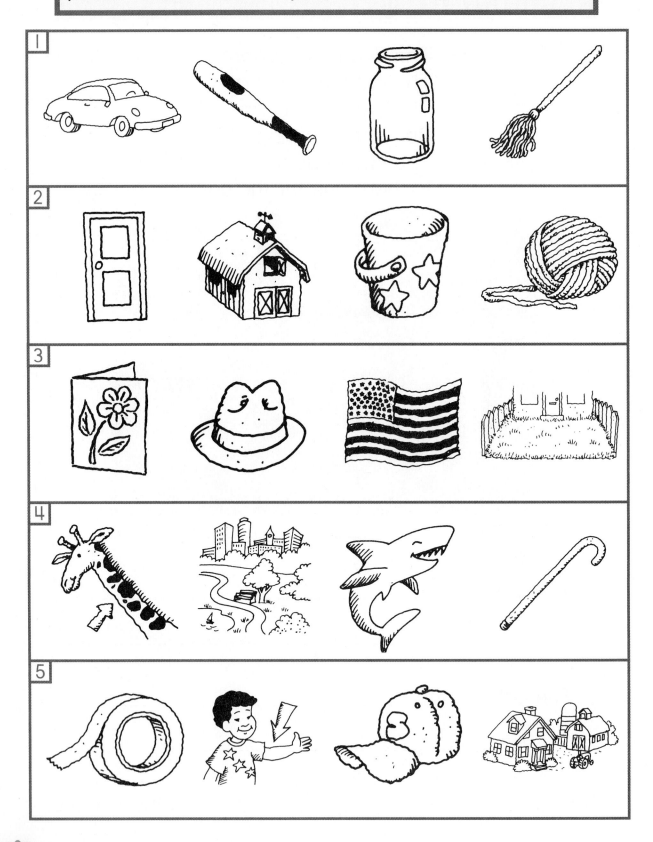

R-controlled Vowel: / är / • Phonemic Awareness

Phonics Practice Book

Harcourt

Name _____

Harcourt

Name _____

car

Write **ar** to complete each picture name that has the vowel sound /är/. Then trace the rest of the word.

1	2	3
t ar	c p	c t

4	5	6
sh k	b n	h t

7	8	9
n l	m	st

10	11	12
c n	c d	p k

Name _____

Write the name of each picture.

1  bar	2 	3
4	5	6
7 	8 	9 

tar

Write the picture names that rhyme with **tar**.
Then add one more rhyming word and a picture.

1

_____

tar

2

_____

3

_____

4

_____

R-controlled Vowel: / är / *ar* • Phonograms   Phonics Practice Book

Harcourt

Slide and read the word. Then color the picture it names.

1   **b a r n**

2   **p a r k**

3   **s t a r**

4   **c a r t**

5   **c a r**

Name _____

Write the word that completes each sentence.

| park | car | barn | card | hard | farm |

1

_____

It would be _____ to find a better friend than Mark.

2

We played in the

_____

_____ a lot.

3

Now his home is on a

_____

_____ .

4

Mark likes to help in the

_____

_____ .

5

We will go there in our

_____

_____ .

6

For now, I will send a

_____

_____ to Mark.

Harcourt

Name _____

Do what the sentences tell you.

1. Spark barks a lot.  Color Spark.

2. Find the horse, Star. Put a cart next to Star.

3. Clark parks his car next to the barn.  Color the car.

4. Find the one with a scarf.  Color the scarf red.

5. Karl will dig on the farm.  Color Karl's pants.

Color each picture whose name has the vowel sound /ûr/.

1	2	3

4	5	6

7	8	9

R-controlled Vowel: / ûr /   •   Phonemic Awareness

Phonics Practice Book

Harcourt

Name _____

her

Write **er** to complete each picture name that has the vowel sound /ûr/. Then trace the rest of the word.

1	2	3
h ___ d	b ___ ll	f ___ n

stir

Write **ir** to complete each picture name that has the vowel sound /ûr/. Then trace the rest of the word.

4	5	6
p ___ g	b ___ d	g ___ l

curb

Write **ur** to complete each picture name that has the vowel sound /ûr/. Then trace the rest of the word.

7	8	9
h ___ t	t ___ n	s ___ n

Harcourt

Name _____

Say the name of each picture. Circle the letters that stand for the vowel sound. Then write the name of the picture.

1.
u
(ur)
ar

curb

2.
or
e
ir

3.
ir
or
u

4.
ar
er
o

5.
e
ar
ur

6.
ir
o
or

7.
ar
er
a

8.
or
ar
ir

9.
ur
a
ar

R-controlled Vowel: / ûr / *er*, *ir*, *ur* • Writing Words

Phonics Practice Book

Name _____

churn

Write the picture names that rhyme with **churn**.

1	2

_____	_____

skirt

Write the picture names that rhyme with **skirt**.

3	4

_____	_____

R-controlled Vowel: / ûr / *er, ir, ur* • Phonograms

Name _____

1. hurt

2. bird

3. fern

4. shirt

5. turn

R-controlled Vowel: / ûr / *er, ir, ur* • Blending

Phonics Practice Book

Harcourt

Name _____

Write **er** to complete each word. Then trace the rest of the word and draw a picture for the word.

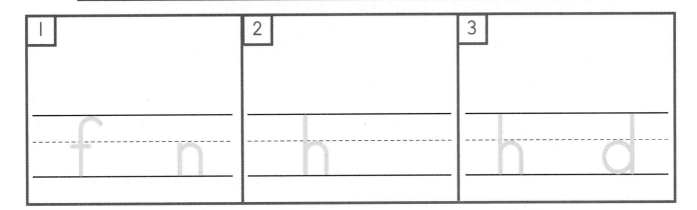

1	2	3
f ___ n	h ___	h ___ d

Write **ir** to complete each word. Then trace the rest of the word and draw a picture for the word.

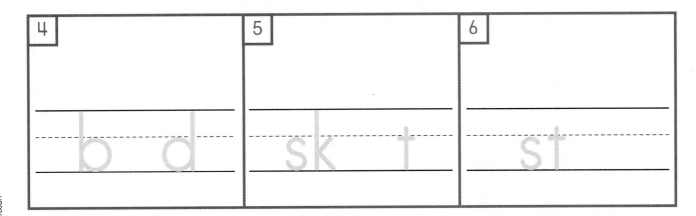

4	5	6
b ___ d	sk ___ t	___ st

Write **ur** to complete each word. Then trace the rest of the word and draw a picture for the word.

7	8	9
c ___ l	___ t n	t ___ tle

Harcourt

Name _____

Write the word that completes each sentence.

fur   skirt   purple   turn   shirt   her

1		Bert put on his _____ ------------------------- _____ .
2		_____ ------------------------- Fern put on _____ socks.
3		_____ ------------------------- Gert has a _____ .
4		We all have on _____ ------------------------- _____ !
5		_____ ------------------------- Look at her _____ .
6		_____ ------------------------- She wants to _____ purple, too!

272

R-controlled Vowel: / ûr / *er*, *ir*, *ur* • Reading Words

Phonics Practice Book

Name _____

Do what the sentences tell you.

1. Kurt got there first. Put a **1** on Kurt's shirt.

2. Do you see the turtle in the ferns? Color the turtle.

3. Color the girl's shirt purple.

4. Color the bird that chirps.

5. Herb stirs. Put an **H** on Herb's shirt.

Name _____

Write the word that names each picture.

star	herd	curl	cart	fern	card
dirt	bird	arm	barn	girl	turn

1. _____

2. _____

3. _____

4. _____

5. _____

6. _____

7. _____

8. _____

9. _____

10. _____

11. _____

12. _____

Review of *R*-controlled Vowels: / är / *ar;* / ûr / *er, ir, ur*

Phonics Practice Book

Name _____

Circle and write the word that completes each sentence.

1	This is for my _____ _____ !	bark bird bed
2	Put it in the _____ _____ .	cart cat curl
3	It's our _____ _____ next.	tar turn ten
4	Carl is the _____ _____ .	class click clerk
5	I'll put it in the _____ _____ .	corn car can
6	It is getting _____ _____ out.	dirt dark desk

Harcourt

Name _____

Underline the word that answers the question. Then write the word.

1		Hurt or a horn?	
2		Stir or a star?	
3		A fort or a fern?	
4		A fork or a farm?	
5		A shirt or a shark?	
6		A storm or a start?	
7		A bird or a barn?	
8		Corn or a curb?	

Harcourt

Name _____

A Long Walk

Mark and his dad started to walk along a path. At first they saw a lot of ferns. They saw birds and a big turtle. Mark's shirt got torn on a sharp thorn, but the thorn did not hurt his arm. A storm started, so they ran into an old barn.

At last they got back to where the car was parked. By then it was getting dark. They had walked far! Mark and his dad had some popcorn and looked at the stars.

1. What did Mark and his dad see?

_____

_____

_____

_____

2. What did they do when the storm started?

_____

_____

_____

3. What did they look at when they had popcorn?

_____

_____

_____

Harcourt

Fill in the circle next to the name of the picture.

1
- ○ star
- ○ stir
- ○ stop

2
- ○ bit
- ○ bark
- ○ bird

3
- ○ curl
- ○ cart
- ○ cork

4
- ○ curb
- ○ corn
- ○ car

5
- ○ port
- ○ park
- ○ pick

6
- ○ fern
- ○ farm
- ○ fort

7
- ○ bed
- ○ bat
- ○ bar

8
- ○ torn
- ○ tar
- ○ turn

9
- ○ short
- ○ shirt
- ○ sharp

10
- ○ card
- ○ cork
- ○ cot

11
- ○ gas
- ○ get
- ○ girl

12
- ○ stamp
- ○ storm
- ○ start

Harcourt

R-controlled Vowels Test

Phonics Practice Book

Name _____

Fill in the circle next to the sentence that tells about the picture.

1		
		○ They find forks in a barn.
		○ They pick corn on a farm.
		○ They see cars by the curb.

2		
		○ The dogs see a cart in the yard.
		○ The dogs start going north.
		○ The dogs bark at the stars.

3		
		○ This bird can see in the dark.
		○ This shirt got torn.
		○ The storm will start now.

4		
		○ The thorns are purple.
		○ The bird has no horns.
		○ The turtle has no fur.

5		
		○ Make a mark on the chart.
		○ Turn the short one now.
		○ Stir this with your fork.

6		
		○ That cork goes back and forth.
		○ They march in the ferns.
		○ The first one has a horn.

Harcourt

Name _____

Write **ow** for each picture whose name has the vowel sound /ou/. Then trace the rest of the word.

1.

_____
c _ _ _ _ _

2.

_____
cl _ _ _ n

3.

_____
f _ _ ld

4.

_____
cr _ _ d

5.

_____
b _ _

6.

_____
t _ _ st

7.

_____
cr _ _ n

8.

_____
t _ _ n

Vowel Variant: / ou / *ow*

Phonics Practice Book

Harcourt

Circle the word that completes each sentence. Then write the word.

1		We like to go to _____ ------------------------ _____.	team town ten
2		Why is there a _____ ------------------------ _____?	crop crate crowd
3		Look! It's a _____ ------------------------ _____!	clean clown clam
4		_____ ------------------------ That's _____ he goes so high.	how hop hide
5		_____ ------------------------ Up and _____ he jumps.	dime dock down
6		Now he takes a _____ ------------------------ _____.	bee bow bag

Harcourt

Name _____

Look at each picture and read the sentence. Write the contraction that stands for the underlined words.

**Tim is =
Tim's**

**Pat is =
Pat's**

**It is =
It's**

**What is =
What's**

1

Pat is looking for cookies.

_____

_____ looking for cookies.

2

Tim is looking for cookies, too.

_____

_____ looking for cookies, too.

3

What is in this pan?

_____

_____ in this pan?

4

Surprise! It is a ham!

_____

Surprise! _____ a ham!

Contraction: 's

Phonics Practice Book

Name _____

Look at each picture and read the sentence. Write the contraction that stands for the underlined words.

**can not =
can't**

**did not =
didn't**

**is not =
isn't**

**do not =
don't**

| 1 |  | Dan <u>can not</u> see the big apple. _____ -------------------- Dan _____ see the big apple. |

| 2 | | Tom hid it, but <u>do not</u> look. _____ -------------------- Tom hid it, but _____ look. |

| 3 | | Dan <u>did not</u> see it at all. _____ -------------------- Dan _____ see it at all. |

| 4 |  | Now the apple <u>is not</u> big. _____ -------------------- Now the apple _____ big. |

Contraction: *n't*

Name _____

Color the block if the contraction stands for the two words below it.

1. don't
is not

2. she's
she is

3. what's
what is

4. can't
can not

5. don't
do not

6. he's
she is

7. isn't
is not

8. it's
it is

9. didn't
did not

Harcourt

Name _____

Look at each picture and read the sentence. Write the contraction that stands for the underlined words.

I will =
I'll

She will =
She'll

You will =
You'll

We will =
We'll

1 	<u>She will</u> be glad we are here. _____ ---------------------------------- _____ be glad we are here.	
2 	<u>I will</u> help you pop it. _____ ---------------------------------- _____ help you pop it.	
3 	<u>We will</u> help you, too. _____ ---------------------------------- _____ help you, too.	
4	<u>You will</u> eat it all! _____ ---------------------------------- _____ eat it all!	

Harcourt

Name _____

Look at each picture and read the sentence. Write the contraction that stands for the underlined words.

 I have = I've

 We have = We've

 They are = They're

 You are = You're

| 1 |  | We have played all day.
_____
- -
_____ played all day. |

| 2 |  | You are hot and tired.
_____
- -
_____ hot and tired. |

| 3 | | I have had a rest now.
_____
- - - - - - - - - - - - - - - - -
_____ had a rest now. |

| 4 |  | They are going again.
_____
- -
_____ going again. |

Contractions: 've, 're

Phonics Practice Book

Harcourt

Name _____

Look at each picture, and read the sentence. Write the contraction that stands for the underlined words.

I would = I'd	they would = they'd
we have = we've	you are = you're

1

You are not going to sit down, are you?
_____
- -
_____ not going
to sit down, are you?

2

Yes, we have danced all night.
_____
- - - - - - - - - - - - - - -
Yes,_____ danced all night.

3

But I would like to dance more.
_____
- - - - - - - - - - - -
But _____ like to dance more.

4

I wish they would dance with me!
_____
- - - - - - - - - - - - - - - - - - -
I wish _____ dance
with me!

Harcourt

Name _____

Color the hat if the contraction stands for the two words below it.

1. you've
you have

2. we're
we would

3. they'd
they had

4. I'll
I will

5. it's
it is

6. you'd
we would

7. she's
they are

8. can't
can not

9. he'll
he will

10. didn't
is not

11. I've
I would

12. you're
you are

Harcourt

Cumulative Review of Contractions

Phonics Practice Book

Name _____

Read each sentence. Fill in the circle next to the two words the contraction stands for.

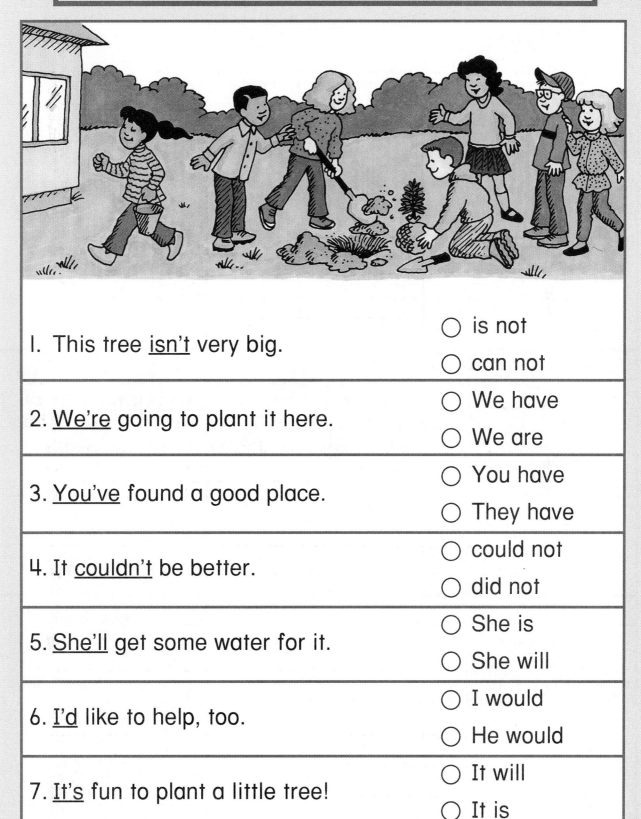

1. This tree <u>isn't</u> very big.
   - ○ is not
   - ○ can not

2. <u>We're</u> going to plant it here.
   - ○ We have
   - ○ We are

3. <u>You've</u> found a good place.
   - ○ You have
   - ○ They have

4. It <u>couldn't</u> be better.
   - ○ could not
   - ○ did not

5. <u>She'll</u> get some water for it.
   - ○ She is
   - ○ She will

6. <u>I'd</u> like to help, too.
   - ○ I would
   - ○ He would

7. <u>It's</u> fun to plant a little tree!
   - ○ It will
   - ○ It is

Harcourt

Name _____

cat

cats

If a picture shows more than one, add **s** to its name. Then trace the whole word.

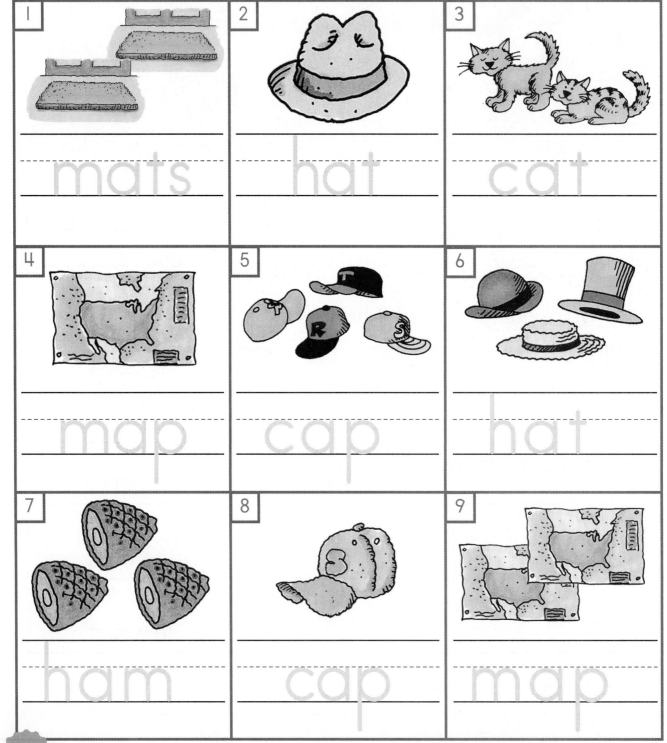

1. mats

2. hat

3. cat

4. map

5. cap

6. hat

7. ham

8. cap

9. map

Inflection: -s

Phonics Practice Book

Harcourt

Name _____

Add **s** to each word to make it tell about now. Then trace the rest of the word.

 The cat look_s_.

1. Pam _come_____ .

2. Ann _pat_____ a cat.

3. Sam _look_____ .

4. Matt _tap_____ .

Use a telling word with **s** in a sentence.

_____

- -

_____

Name _____

Now

I **pick** an apple.

Past

I **picked** an apple.

Add **ed** to each word to make it tell about the past. Then trace the rest of the word.

1. call

2. kick

3. pack

4. look

Now write two sentences about something that happened in the past. Use words with **ed.**

_____

- -

_____

_____

- -

Inflection: -ed

Phonics Practice Book

Harcourt

Name _____

Find three words in the puzzle that end in **ed** and tell about the past. Circle the words. Then write the word from the puzzle that completes each sentence.

h	c	a	l	l	e	d
k	a	m	a	s	p	a
i	l	a	n	d	e	d
c	l	i	d	h	t	s
k	i	c	k	e	d	m

1

_____
- - - - - - - - - - - - - - - - - - -

You _____ it.

2

_____
- - - - - - - - - - - - - - - - - - -

Tim _____

the dog.

3

_____
- - - - - - - - - - - - - - - - - - -

It _____ here.

Harcourt

Name _____

I kick. **I am kicking.**

Add **ing** to each word to make a new word. Then trace the rest of the word.

1	2
pick	look
3	4
call	pack

Now write two sentences that use **ing** words.

_____

_____

_____

_____

Inflection: -ing

Phonics Practice Book

Harcourt

Circle and write the word that completes each sentence.

1	Do you see me _____ ------------------------ _____ it?	kicks kicking kicked
2	_____ ------------------------ Tim is _____ .	picking picks picked
3	Tim is _____ ------------------------ _____ .	packs packed packing
4	_____ ------------------------ Pam is _____ for the cat.	look looking looks
5	_____ ------------------------ Pam is _____ the cat.	calling calls called

Harcourt

Name _____

Circle and write the word that completes each sentence.

1		The _____ had Nat's cap.	cat cats can
2		Nat _____ for the cap.	looking look looks
3		Pam _____ Nat.	calling comes called
4		Pam is _____ on Nat's cap!	sit sits sitting

Review of Inflections: -s, -ed, -ing

Phonics Practice Book

Harcourt

Name _____

Double the final letter of most words with short vowels before adding **ed.**
Double the final consonant and add **ed** to each word.
Then trace the rest of the word.

 pop + p + ed = popped

1	2
_____ hopped	_____ pat

3	4
_____ mop	_____ tag

5	6
_____ stop	_____ skip

Harcourt

Name_____

Circle the word that completes the sentence. Then write the word.

1		pat
	Dan _____ Tip.	patted
		packed

2		hopped
	Tip _____ up on Dan.	hop
		here

3	Dan _____.	slip
		sit
		slipped

4	Dan and Tip _____ for a dip.	stopped
		stops
		stack

Harcourt

Name _____

Double the final consonant of most words with short vowels before adding **ing.**

Double the final consonant and add **ing** to each word. Then trace the rest of the word.

  pop + p + ing = popping

1	2
_____ sitting	_____ hop

3	4
_____ nap	_____ pat

5	6
_____ hit	_____ dig

Name _____

Read the rhyme. Then answer the question.

Go, Friends, Go!

Friends are nodding
  and tapping.
Hands are snapping
  and clapping.
Friends are spinning
  and dipping.
Friends are tipping
  and skipping.

We are hopping.
We are not stopping!

What are the friends doing?

_____

_____

_____

Inflection: -ing • Reading Words in Context

Phonics Practice Book

Harcourt

Name _____

two dish<u>es</u>

dish + es = dishes

He dish<u>es</u> out popcorn.

If a word ends with **sh** or **ss,** add **es** to tell about more than one or to tell about now.

Write **es** to make each picture name tell about more than one. Then trace the rest of the word.

1		2	
glass		dish	

3		4	
ash		lash	

Write the word that completes each sentence.

(dashes   kisses   crashes)

5		
	Mom _____ him.	

6		
	She _____ home.	

Phonics Practice Book   Inflection: -es   301

Name _____

Add **es** to the words. Then use the words you wrote to complete the sentences.

glass
_____

_____

wish
_____

_____

dish
_____

_____

pass
_____

_____

_____

----

1. Ann put milk in the _____ .

_____

----

2. Ron gets the _____ .

_____

----

3. Ann _____ the cookies.

_____

----

4. Tag _____ he could eat one.

Inflection: -es

Phonics Practice Book

Name _____

Circle the word that completes each sentence. Then write the word.

1	_____ - - - - - - - - - - - - - - - - - Nan is _____ with Bob.	spinning sitting swimming
2	_____ - - - - - - - - - - - - - - - - - They _____ at Rick's house.	stopped sipped snapped
3	Rick's dog _____ - - - - - - - - - - - - - - - - - _____ them.	misses dishes passes
4	_____ - - - - - - - - - - - - - - - - - Bob _____ the dog will stop.	wishes ashes hisses
5	_____ - - - - - - - - - - - - - - - - - It _____ into its hole.	hissed hopped hogged

Harcourt

Name _____

Add **er** to each word. Then trace the rest of the word.
Circle the one in each picture that the word tells about.

1
fast

2
sweet

Add **est** to each word. Then trace the rest of the word.
Circle the one in each picture that the word tells about.

3
tall

4

Inflections: -er, -est

Phonics Practice Book

Harcourt

Name _____

Circle and write the word that completes each sentence.

1	_____ The truck is _____ than the car.	big biggest bigger
2	The green truck is _____ _____ than the red one.	taller tall tallest
3	That truck is the _____ _____ of them all.	fast fastest faster
4	What car is the _____ _____ ?	older old oldest
5	_____ My car is _____ than your car.	smallest smaller small

Name _____

Add **es** to some words to tell about more than one. If a word ends with **y**, change the **y** to **i** before adding **es.**

Look at the word that tells about one. Change the **y** to **i** and add **es** to write a word that tells about more than one.

1   family   families

2   baby   _____

Add **es** to some words that tell about now. If a word ends with **y**, change the **y** to **i** before adding **es.**

Look at the word that tells about now. Change the **y** to **i** and add **es** to write a word that tells about now.

3   **They fly.**   It _____.

4   **They try.**   He _____.

Circle and write the word that completes each sentence.

1	Two _____ Two _____ see the tiger.	family families fast
2	Two of them are _____ _____.	babies bats baby
3	_____ A bird _____ to land on one cub.	tried try trying
4	The baby tiger _____ _____.	jump jumps jumping
5	_____ The bird _____ away.	fly flies finds

Harcourt

When a word ends with **e**, drop the **e** before adding **ed**.
Write words that tell about the past. Drop the **e** and add
ed to each word.

chase − e + ed = chased

1 **chase**	2 **wave**	3 **close**
chased		
4 **like**	5 **hope**	6 **joke**
7 **dance**	8 **skate**	9 **trade**

Inflection: *-ed*

Phonics Practice Book

Harcourt

Name _____

Add **ed** to the words below to make them tell about the past.

move	hope
_____	_____
- - - - - - - - - - - - - -	- - - - - - - - - - - - - -
_____	_____
surprise	**dance**
_____	_____
- - - - - - - - - - - - - -	- - - - - - - - - - - - - -
_____	_____

Now use the words you wrote to complete the story.

The Day of the Ducks
_____
- - - - - - - - - - - - - - - - - - - -

1. One day some ducks _____ into a house.

_____
- - - - - - - - - - - - - - - - - -

2. That _____ me!

_____
- - - - - - - - - - - - - - - - - -

3. Three little ducks _____ together.

_____
- - - - - - - - - - - - - - - - - -

4. I _____ we could all be friends.

Harcourt

Name_____

When a word ends with **e**, drop the **e** before adding **ing**. Write new words that tell about now. Drop the **e** and add **ing** to each word.

chase – e + ing = chasing

1 chase	2 trade	3 ride
chasing		

4 wave	5 joke	6 come

7 dance	8 close	9 give

Name _____

Add **ing** to the words below. Then use the words you wrote to complete the sentences.

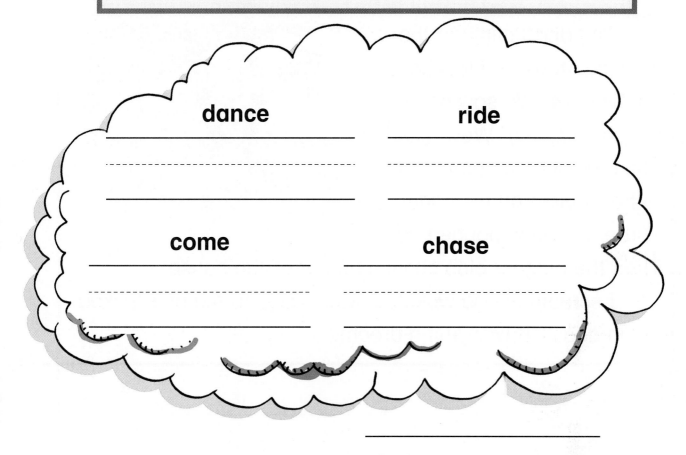

dance

_____

- -

_____

ride

_____

- -

_____

come

_____

- -

_____

chase

_____

- -

_____

_____

- -

1. Look! My book friends are _____ out.

_____

- - - - - - - - - - - - - - - - - - -

2. One is _____ a horse.

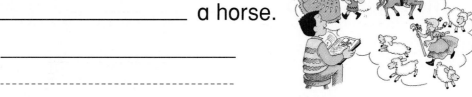

_____

- - - - - - - - - - - - - - - - - - -

3. One is _____ her sheep.

_____

- - - - - - - - - - - - - - - - - - -

4. One is _____ with a mouse.

Name_____

Tim and I climbed the sagging steps and looked in the window. We saw boxes and lots of dust. We walked in. The creaking scared us. Tim felt a tapping on his hand. Three big blobs popped up. Then the biggest blob chased us out of the house!

I screamed and woke up. Mom hugged me and tucked me in again. It was just a dream.

_____
- -

1. The house's steps were _____ .

_____
- -

2. The biggest blob _____ the children.

_____
- -

3. The girl's mother _____ her and

_____
- -

_____ her in.

Cumulative Review: Inflections

Phonics Practice Book

Name _____

1			
		The friends _____ _____ _____ all day.	planted put played
2		Some of them _____ _____ _____ .	hoped hopped helped
3		And some of them _____ _____ _____ .	danced drilled dripped
4		Then they were _____ _____ _____ down.	sitting sliding stopping
5		This one is the _____ _____ _____ .	houses helps highest

Harcourt

Name _____

Fill in the circle next to the word that completes each sentence. Then write the word.

1	We are _____ snacks.	○ makes ○ make ○ making
2	Why is mine _____ _____ than yours?	○ thinner ○ thinking ○ thin
3	I am _____ more in mine.	○ put ○ puffs ○ putting
4	Now mine is the _____ _____ of all.	○ thick ○ thickest ○ tighter
5	You _____ to get too much in there.	○ try ○ tripping ○ tried
6	Oh no! It all _____ _____ out!	○ pop ○ popped ○ poking

Harcourt

Name _____

Add **ed** and **ing** to each word. You may need to add or drop letters.

	+ed	**+ing**
1. like		
2. hop		
3. drip		

Write **s** or **es** to make each word tell about more than one. Then trace the rest of the word.

4	5	6
glass	tree	dish

7	8	9
rake	cat	dress

Harcourt

Cut-Out Fold-Up Books

A Country Dusk

1

Other birds fly up to the trees. They settle onto the branches.

3

Snuggle in. Drift off to sleep. All grows still. It's time to dream.

8

It's time to make the last catch. Skip home before it gets dark.

6

Harcourt

Directions: Help your child cut out and fold the book.   Cut-Out, Fold-Up Book I · Consonant Blends and Digraphs

317

4

Hungry rabbits munch on sweet plants.

2

Hens cluck to their chicks.
Quick, quick. Don't be slow.

Harcourt

Fold

Fold

Frogs splash in for one last swim.

The last flash from the sun fades. It is dusk. Hush, hush.

5

7

Cut-Out, Fold-Up Book 1 · Consonant Blends and Digraphs

Directions: Help your child cut out and fold the book.

Where IS Pat?

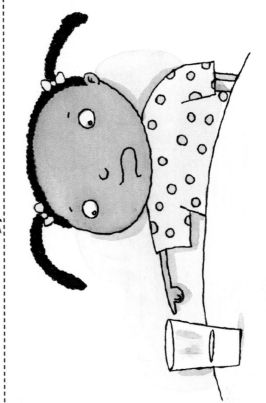

Did Pat sit here?

Did Pat sip this?

Harcourt

---Fold---

---Fold---

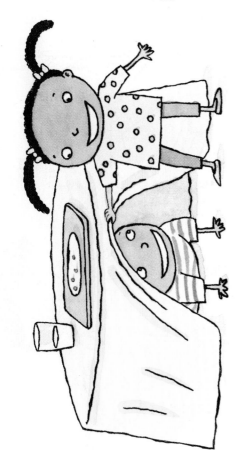

Pat is here!

Pat hid.

Did Pat come here?

Pat? Pat?

Directions: Help your child cut out and fold the book.

Cut-Out, Fold-Up Book 2 • Short Vowels: *a, i*

Did Dad see Pat?
Did Tim see him?

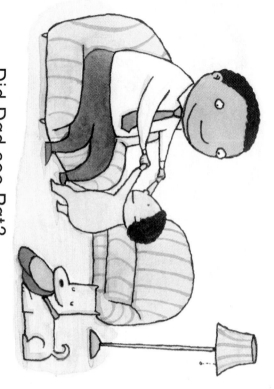

—Fold—

2

Where is Pat?
Is Pat here?

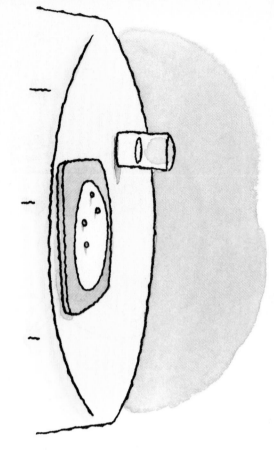

Harcourt

—Fold—

Sam has a cap.
It is Pat's cap!

Look at this, Pam.
Pat sat here.

Cut-Out, Fold-Up Book 2 • Short Vowels: *a, i*

Directions: Help your child cut out and fold the book.

Bob Bug's Big Pet

—Fold—

Rocks do not run or eat bugs. "A rock is the best pet for me!" said Bob.

But a hen needs a nest. A hen makes too much mess.

—Fold—

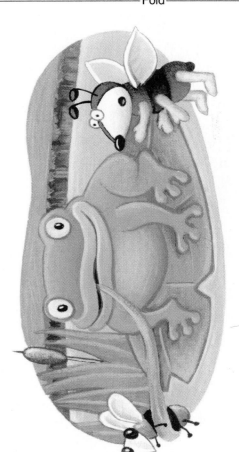

A frog hops and eats bugs. A frog is not a good pet for a bug!

Directions: Help your child cut out and fold the book.

Cut-Out, Fold-Up Book 3 · Short Vowels: *o, e, u*

A duck needs a pond. It's not fun for a bug to get wet!

Bob Bug sets out to get a big pet. "What if I got a pet hen?" said Bob.

Harcourt

—Fold—

—Fold—

Bob spots a fox. A fox runs too fast.

Bob rests on a rock in the sun. Rocks do not need nests or ponds.

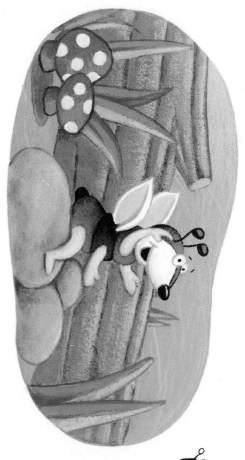

Cut-Out, Fold-Up Book 3 • Short Vowels: *o, e, u*

Directions: Help your child cut out and fold the book.

Kelly and Kate

Over the field and down the trail, they run to the lake to see the boats sail.

3

Kelly and Kate, before it's too late, run on home and open the gate.

Harcourt

8

Reach for peaches on Miss Annie's tree.
A peach for you, a leaf for me!

6

Directions: Help your child cut out and fold the book.

Cut-Out, Fold-Up Book 4 • Long Vowels: *e, a*

4

It's too chilly to wade in the lake so they walk by the trees in the shade.

2

Kelly and Kate race out to play on a sunny, breezy day.

Fold

Fold

Harcourt

Kate and Kelly leap down a lane, peek into a cave, and wave to a train.

5

Places to go, games to play— The girls have so much to see and say.

7

Might

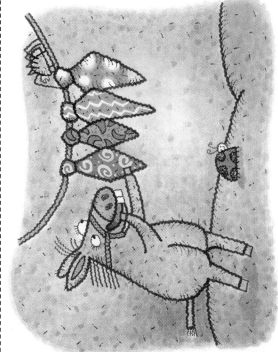

"I might," said my mule,
"if I find the right tie."

Harcourt

Fold

Fold

"Would you like to go on a TV show?"
"Oh, no!" they cry. "We're all too shy!"

8

Would a goat play a tune
on a flute in the snow?

6

Directions: Help your child cut out and fold the book.

Cut-Out, Fold-Up Book 5 · Long Vowels: *o, i, u*

4

Would a mole shine his bike
and ride by to say hi?

2

Would my mule go a mile
to see a toad try to fly?

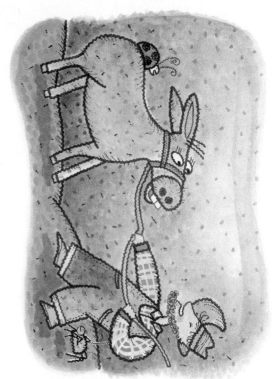

—Fold—

—Fold—

"I might," sighed the mole,
"if you hold my lime pie."

5

"I might," said the goat,
"if my nose isn't cold."

7

Cut-Out, Fold-Up Book 5 • Long Vowels: *o, i, u*

Directions: Help your child cut out and fold the book.

Barb's Farm

1

"It couldn't hurt to get some birds," said Barb.

3

"It couldn't hurt to get some turtles," said Barb.

8

Birds chirped in the yard, on her skirt, or on her arms.

6

Harcourt

Directions: Help your child cut out and fold the book.

Cut-Out, Fold-Up Book 6 • *R*-Controlled Vowels

327

4

Corn is good for birds.
But then the birds started
to eat her ferns.

2

Barb's farm had a big red barn
that was bursting with corn.

Fold

Fold

Birds perched in the
barn, on the porch,
and in her car.

Harcourt

It was hard to part with them.
But Barb's birds had to go.

5

7

Cut-Out, Fold-Up Book 6 · *R*-Controlled Vowels

Directions: Help your child cut out and fold the book.

1

Harcourt

Fold

It's a big place, isn't it?

There's a lot to see here.

3

Fold

I hope you've had a good time.

Aren't you glad you came?

8

Now I'd like to see the whales.

They're even bigger than these fish.

9

She's giving us maps so
we'll know where we're going.

We're taking a class trip.
Come with us, and we'll have fun.

—Fold—

Harcourt

—Fold—

Don't you feel like we've dived
into the sea? But we're not wet!

I didn't know they'd do tricks!
She'll give them treats.

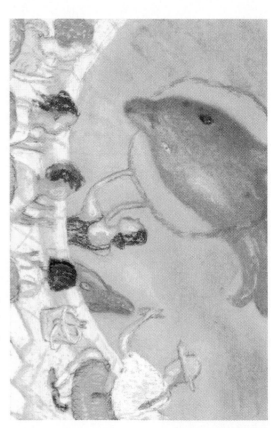

Cut-Out, Fold-Up Book 7 · Contractions

Directions: Help your child cut out and fold the book.